DEDICATION

TO GOD:
ALL GLORY, PRAISE AND HONOR;
and thanksgiving for
the blessing of Charlie.

∼∽∼

THE
AMERICAN
PRAYER BOOK

In GOD We Trust

Reflections, prayers, and suggested actions to celebrate important dates in the American and Christian calendar.

●

Marci Alborghetti

CATHOLIC BOOK PUBLISHING CORP.
New Jersey

NIHIL OBSTAT: Rev. Donald E. Blumenfeld, Ph.D.
Censor Librorum

IMPRIMATUR: ✠ Most Rev. John J. Myers. J.C.D., D.D.
Archbishop of Newark

(T-924)

ISBN 978-1-937913-25-0

© 2012 Catholic Book Publishing Corp., New Jersey
Printed in the USA
www.catholicbookpublishing.com

Contents

INTRODUCTION

ACCORDING to the nurses at the hospital where I was born, I was the fourth baby girl to be born at 4:44 in the morning on the Fourth of July. I have known this for as long as I can remember, and I'm sure my mother told me, though she never said whether that distinguishing fact applied to the hospital, my home state of Connecticut or the country I was blessed to be born in. It never seemed very important.

Want more on my patriotic roots? I turned sweet sixteen on the nation's Bicentennial and 40 at the turn of the century. When I was little, my grandfather used to come to our house around dawn so that he could set a firecracker off under my window at precisely 4:44 a.m. At church fairs in the summer I would always bet on 4 when the wheel spun, and I ended up with more stuffed animals and useless prizes than I knew what to do with. Every birthday cake I've ever had has been decorated with red, white, and blue sugar candies or frosting. And, no, I'm not foolish enough to have the number 4 in any pin number for any card or account I own!

So naturally, I am a red, white, and blue patriot, a my-country-right-or-wrong kind of person, right?

Not exactly.

From the very first time Sister Jacinta, my first grade teacher, pointed to the Crucifix hanging on the wall in the front of our classroom and said, "Remember, children, that Jesus died for our sins," I've been acutely aware of the concept of sin; exceedingly conscious of the sometimes barely discernible difference between right and wrong. And perhaps because I felt, even as a young girl, so tied to America because of our shared birthday, as I became aware of right and wrong for myself, I grew increasingly aware of it for my country. I knew that when I sinned by wronging someone else and offending God, I needed to seek and accept forgiveness, a process that often to our chagrin, requires humility. This, I believed, was my responsibility; the very least I owed God for my existence: repentance and, whenever possible, some restitution.

By the same token, I grew up believing that when America did wrong, it ought to admit it, seek God's forgiveness, and try to make up for the wrong. I've learned that this is not the way everyone views our country. Some of us believe that showing humility and seeking forgiveness are intolerable expressions of weakness that America must never demonstrate.

Even with my extraordinary birth-tie to our nation, I don't think it's unpatriotic to want the best from my country, because I know that America has been so blessed by God that it can afford to strive to do the best and be the best. In fact, I believe it is downright patriotic to admit when we've done wrong, seek God's forgiveness, and try to make up for our missteps. Just as I think I owe God my confession, repentance and restitution, I think America owes God—and the world—the same.

Make no mistake, we are a great country. And, as Jesus said, where much is given, much is required. The United States of America, as we will see in the coming pages, is a noble, magnificent, and amazing work-in-progress. There has never been a nation like it; and that is why we are held to a greater standard. That is why we must hold *ourselves* to a greater standard. We have raised the bar high, and when we sneak under it, God and the world and our own people know it. No amount of posturing or hubris can hide it.

I don't think for one moment that God wants me to give in to a sense of complacency, to stop seeking His will and His forgiveness when I fail. I feel the same way about the country whose birthday He allowed me to share. The reflections, prayers, and suggested actions in the pages that follow—each corresponding to important days and holidays in the American and Christian calendar—reflect my passion for my country and for its potential in the context of my love for, awe of, and faith in God. I hope my readers share my feelings for God and country and that praying through the commemorative dates each year with me will bless them and the great nation we are blessed to occupy.

Prayer on a National Holiday

HEAVENLY Father,
   You created me and made me
a citizen of this country
by birth (or by naturalization).
Let me take part in this holiday
with joy and gratitude.
As I am renewed in mind and body,
may I also be refreshed in spirit.
Make me take this occasion
to rededicate myself to my country
to lovingly uphold its legitimate traditions,
readily obey its decent laws,
and show genuine concern for its people.
At the same time, may I bear uncompromis-
      ing witness
of my Christian Faith to my fellow citizens
and to those who may not be followers of
      Jesus.

JANUARY 1

NEW YEAR'S DAY

IN theory, New Year's Day for Americans should represent the classic fresh start. It is the first day of the month, the first day of the year, the crest of winter. There should be a purity to the day, and in testimony to this, it is the day that Catholics celebrate the solemnity of Mary, the Mother of God. New Year's Day should awaken in us a sense of renewal, another chance to try to get it right, as individuals, as Christians, as Americans.

That's the theory anyway.

In reality, we often fall all too short of this glorious utopian ideal. The reality is that more than a few of us have likely over-indulged in food and drink and late night revelry the night before. And even the most disciplined among us are at least likely to have consumed too many Christmas goodies over the past week. Maybe we have not kept up with our regular exercise and, most certainly, we have not slept as well or as long as usual over the past days and nights. Most of us have spent more money than we should have, and it is the rare American who makes it to New Year's Day without feeling that it has all been just a little too much.

We've been celebrating. We've been trying to forget, for a few hours or days, our worries and problems. We've tried not to think about our concerns over money, family, or work. We've tried to ignore our fears about the nation's economy, climate change, and the troops engaged in military actions. We've tried to avoid considering our own moral compasses or whether we are still a great and *good* nation.

It is natural to put these things away for a few days at Christmas-time. But now, as my mother used to say, "The party's over." And instead of feeling excited at the prospect of a new year, a new start, a new opportunity to address these issues, we may just feel worn out. We can feel like everything has come crashing down on us during this short, deep-winter day where even if the sun is out, it is probably as weak and tired as we feel. How can we drag our burdens out of the dim corner where we've shoved them and lift them once again onto our shoulders?

I bet God knows just how we feel. We can easily imagine how often He might be dismayed with His creation and what hurts Him in humankind and the world. How easy it would be for Him to simply continue to celebrate among the saints and angels, basking in unknowable glory and adoration!

And yet, He never turns away, not for a season of revel, not for a day, not for an instant. He never releases the burden that is us, our country, the world. He never abandons us or stops giving us chances to start again, to renew our commitment to goodness, to Him. God constantly provides us with the gift of renewal.

Today represents just such a gift. God knows that many of us are not full of vim and vigor this New Year's Day. That's why God sends us His Spirit so that we may exchange our weariness for grace and go out and renew the face of the earth. It is the one gift of this season that we will not have to exchange and will never stop needing.

PRAYER

GOD of all creation, new and old, strengthen us on this new day of this new year. Give us a portion of Your Spirit so that we may cleanse our hearts and souls, preparing to make true New Year resolutions, the kind that will bring us closer to You. Teach us to get our bodies and our souls in shape so that we may do the work You give us this year. Remind us to be grateful for the pleasures You have provided over the past season and year, and prepare us to recognize Your gifts in the year that begins today. Bless our nation and renew in our leaders a spirit of collaboration and justice. Make us, once again, a great and good nation. Amen.

ACTIVITY

MOVE something in a new direction today: your body, your mind, your furniture, something. If you haven't exercised for weeks because of the holidays, get out and take a walk or bike ride. Go to church and park a few blocks away so you can walk the extra distance. Talk to your pastor about the sermon. If the weather is poor, ride an exercise bike, do yoga, or stretching exercises. Move your brain by reading a challenging article or book; doing a word puzzle. Watch a documentary. Start a lively discussion. Write a letter to the editor of your paper or respond with an on-line comment to an article or editorial. Clean out a cupboard. Clean out a closet. Wash your windows (weather permitting). Whatever activity you engage in, whatever part of your life or yourself you decide to move in a new direction, be conscious of the fact that your action represents a new start. It is just the beginning.

SAINT JOHN NEUMANN

JOHN Neumann is a wonderful example of how the United States and Christianity in America have benefited from the riches of many nations and cultures. Born in what was then Bohemia in 1811, Neumann was fascinated with the relatively New World of America and greatly interested in becoming a missionary in the United States. While studying for the priesthood, he obtained permission to come to this country, and he was ordained in New York at the age of 25.

Ambitious and hard-working as any new immigrant, Neumann was nonetheless more dedicated to God's work than he was to his own advancement. He was particularly committed to other immigrants in the United States and to education. Accordingly, in 1842 Neumann was the first American immigrant priest to join the Redemptorist order, and he spent the next ten years working in Pennsylvania, Ohio, and Maryland. In 1852 Neumann was made Bishop of Philadelphia.

Established now with an impressive amount of power, the future saint began to work in earnest within his diocese, focusing on strengthening existing parishes and establishing new parishes, particularly for immigrants who wanted places where they could worship in their own language and follow their own traditions. An immigrant himself, Neumann understood the importance of both a worship community and a good education for new arrivals to America, and he increased the number of Catholic schools in his diocese from 2 to 100. Neumann's zeal and commitment came at the cost of his own health. He died in 1860 shortly before his 49th birthday. On June 19, 1977, Pope Paul VI made John Neumann a saint.

While at once a deeply religious man, John Neumann also reflected the best in American values. From his birthplace in Bohemia, he recognized the United States as a land of opportunity, both for himself and for God's work. He pursued this vision diligently, and, like the most successful of America's leaders, he worked for the good of the community and the nation while simultaneously advancing his own objectives. Neumann also exemplified the church's commitment to immigrants, again from a dual perspective in that Christianity is foremost concerned with the soul of the individual (he could hear confessions in at least six languages), but the Church also realizes that the body and mind must also be nurtured.

This is nothing less than a prescription from Jesus for Christian living: feed the poor, house the homeless, visit the sick and the imprisoned, bring the good news to those who haven't heard it. It is a clear and simple statement from our Lord, but as the state of immigration politics in America today proves, human nature makes it seem very complicated!

America has always had an uneasy relationship with its immigrants, which is rather strange since nearly all Americans are either immigrants or descended from immigrants, many of whom were seeking to escape the strictures of life in their place of origin. Yet for all that America is truly a melting pot, more than a few groups have been badly burned before they were able to melt into the stew. We see this today in America, and once again, as in the time of Saint John Neumann, Christian leaders are often the first ones to advocate for the newest wave of immigrants to this country.

PRAYER

FATHER of many children, we thank You for sending us men and women like John Neumann who understood the challenges facing newcomers because he, himself, experienced them. Please strengthen Your communities in our country, many of which are composed of people who arrived on these shores from other nations, so that they may stand with today's struggling immigrants whether they be rich or poor, educated or unschooled, scientists or laborers, fair-skinned or dark-skinned. Forgive us when we falter in doing the right thing, the Christian thing, and remind us of Jesus' example always. Amen.

ACTIVITY

IN honor of John Neumann, do something to support newcomers to the United States. Many of the latest wave of immigrants are either Eastern European or Latino, and they can often be found in our churches and in service-oriented work. If you know of an immigrant or immigrant family, go out of your way to say a kind or welcoming word. If the person or his/her family are neighbors or fellow parishioners, invite them for coffee or a meal. Explore what your church is doing to support immigrants and offer to get involved. If your church does not have such a program, start a discussion about how your community can help those new to America. Send messages of support to church leaders and politicians who are dealing with immigrants in a Christian manner. Volunteer in a literacy or English-as-a-Second-Language program. Donate food or clothing to a charity that helps immigrants.

JANUARY 6

EPIPHANY, THREE KINGS DAY

IN some countries, and in a number of cities in America, Epiphany is almost as important as Christmas, and not only because it is the day presents are exchanged in some cultures. Traditionally, this 12th day after Christmas marks the arrival of the Three Kings at the Holy Family's humble home. In the United States we celebrate at Mass on the first Sunday following January 6, those three powerful men who came bearing very expensive and royal gifts fit for a king: gold, frankincense, and myrrh.

But that first Epiphany was about much more than mere presents, no matter how priceless and extraordinary. These three wise men, leaders in government and science, had traveled great distances to meet this newborn king. They did not take one look at the impoverished family and turn around to try to find the palace where they were really meant to be. They did not doubt what God had revealed to them through portents in the dome over the earth called the sky. They knelt each in turn, humbling themselves, and laid their fantastic gifts before the sturdy crib built by a carpenter foster father.

What really happened that day? This was so much more than "the first Christmas presents," as we're often told. This was government and science acknowledging the birth of Jesus! This was the leadership of nations humbling itself before the Son of God! Imagine this! It is likely that these men had paid their respects to the sons of kings before this day; likely that they had entered ornate palaces and been ushered through marble and tile corridors to enter a nursery well-attended by guards and beautifully robed servants, sparkling with gold and silver and gems, to leave their gifts of acknowledgment. It is likely that they had often done the politically correct thing and congratulated the king over the birth of his handsome son who would someday rule the principality. It is likely that they often departed, relieved to have the ritual over with, and talking among themselves about political maneuverings, necessary alliances, and the quality of tribal government.

But, nothing in the experience of those three wise men would have prepared them to pay obeisance to a child swaddled in rags and watched over by a young peasant girl and her humble husband. Nothing had readied them for their initial astonishment and then dawning, awed comprehension of who the little Prince before them truly was. As men of science, they had waited for years for that particular light in the sky. As men of government, they had waited throughout their careers for a leader worth following. As men of spirit, they had waited their whole life to find the One to put their faith in, the One who would make sense of the nations and the stars and the heavens because in Him they had their being.

America is a nation founded "under God." We are a people who, like the Three Kings, recognize the majesty, peace and justice of a God in and of Whom is all creation, including this country and every person and every thing in it. We seek leaders willing to bow in humility before the rough-hewn cradle of the Lord. Our Epiphany is continual. We must be constantly and consciously moving toward God, recognizing His power over everything, seeking and bowing to His will in our lives and for our nation.

PRAYER

JESUS, Son of the Father, send the Spirit to us that we may follow the lead of the Three Kings and move diligently toward You in all that we do. Teach us to seek You in humility and hopefulness, and guide us to choose leaders who will do the same. Remind us that what is right for us as Your people is also right for us as Your nation. Let us feel the same reverent wonder that those three bearers of gifts felt when they realized that all things come together in and under You. Let us bring You gifts fitting of that understanding. Amen.

ACTIVITY

THINK about what the wise men must have felt when they first laid eyes on Jesus. Consider what their expectations must have been and then imagine what they thought when they discovered the reality of God. Did they wonder if they'd in fact brought the right gifts? Did they question whether this infant King would have need of such worldly goods? What gift would you bring Jesus? What gift could you lay before the crib that would befit the One you seek to honor? Give this some thought and when you've made a decision, make an effort this year to give that gift to the Lord.

JANUARY 14

ANNIVERSARY OF THE END
OF THE WAR FOR
INDEPENDENCE/TREATY OF PARIS

THE end of the Revolutionary War was relatively calm and courteous as such things
go. Although the United States had won the
war by becoming the first "civilized" people to
use a form of guerrilla warfare, it was nonetheless a time when the conduct of war was pro-
scribed by traditions of behavior that were at
least superficially honorable. And, of course,
so was the conduct of negotiating the peace.
Those were the days!

The comparatively civil end to the American
War for Independence may have had something to do with the fact that, figuratively
speaking, America was like a young adult
at war with an aging parent. And some of
the siblings disagreed about whether there
should have even been a war. Throughout the
Revolutionary War, the American colonies
remained home to men and women who considered themselves just that: British colonists
who remained loyal to—if not always in agree-
ment with—England, but were still unwilling
to fight and kill their fellow colonists. While
the revolutionary colonists emerged the vic-

tors, there were some who never lost sight of their connection to England and the need to form a new, mutually beneficial, relationship.

The Treaty of Paris, which was ratified by The Continental Congress in Annapolis, Maryland, on January 14, 1784, reflected that need for an advantageous peace in both its creation and its elements. After England's defeat, Paris was selected as the ostensibly neutral international city where peace talks would be conducted, beginning in April 1782. Great Britain was represented at the talks by Richard Oswald; the American representatives were the American Peace Commissioners including the wise and wily Benjamin Franklin, the pragmatic John Jay, and the dour, careful John Adams. They were later joined by Henry Laurens. Although the initial articles of peace were signed on November 30, 1782, the actual Treaty of Paris, which officially ended the war, was signed nearly a year later on September 3, 1783. The resulting document revealed the kind of intricate diplomacy at play for the intervening period of almost two years.

The first article, of course, named the Revolutionary War victor: "acknowledging the Thirteen Colonies to be free, sovereign and independent States, and that the British Crown and all heirs and successors relinquish claims to the Government, proprietary, and territorial rights of the same, and every part thereof." But despite that seemingly clear declaration, other articles in the treaty make an acknowledging nod to both Britain and the loyalists still in America. For example, Article 3 granted fishing rights to the United States in the Grand Banks and off the coast of Newfoundland which Article 2 had established as British North America (otherwise known to us as Canada). In an effort to recognize loyalists, Article 5 committed the new American government to "earnestly recommend" that state legislatures "provide for the restitution of all estates, rights, and properties which have been confiscated belonging to real British subjects (Loyalists)." Article 6 further strengthened Article 5 by stating that there would be no future confiscation of Loyalist property. And Article 8, reflecting the eventual close trade collaboration between England and America, called for Great Britain and the United States to each have perpetual access to the Mississippi River.

It is interesting that the Treaty of Paris, one of the founding documents of the United States, is based on collaboration with a former sovereign and enemy. At the earliest point in our history as a nation we understood and acted upon the Christian principles of love and fairness and avoided malicious vindictiveness. From a political perspective this could help to elevate and improve one's own situation. From a Christian perspective, it is simply a matter of obeying God.

PRAYER

JESUS, You taught us to love one another as we love ourselves, to treat "the other" as we would wish to be treated. In government, we come back to this commandment again and again. When we have done it, our life and lot and country have improved. When we have failed to do it, we have failed or been diminished. Lord, remind us that what makes us good Christians also makes us good Americans. Teach us to use our power well. Lead us to be always merciful, and when it seems to us that justice and mercy cannot meet, let us choose mercy . . . as You taught us to do. Amen.

ACTIVITY

IS there someone in your life over whom you hold—or believe you hold—some small power or even a sense of superiority? Have you recently won an argument—or so it may seem to you—with someone? Have you defeated a competitive colleague or peer at work or at school? It may be a spouse, child, co-worker, subordinate, neighbor, parishioner, employee, even friend. Understand that whatever advantage you perceive you have over this person is only an advantage if you use it to lift this person up. And then do so.

JANUARY, THIRD MONDAY
MARTIN LUTHER KING, JR.

Martin Luther King, Jr., might be smiling sadly but knowingly in heaven over the long process of making his birthday a holiday. In many ways, that struggle was a reflection of the one he experienced throughout his entire adult life. Born on January 15, 1929, the Reverend Doctor Martin Luther King, Jr., was struck down by an assassin's bullet in 1968. Although not yet 40 years old, Dr. King was internationally known for his pioneering work in civil rights for African Americans and, eventually, all Americans and citizens of the world. Reverend King became the face of the Civil Rights Movement in this country, eventually expanding his work to include protests against various other global injustices.

An avid student of Gandhi's ultimately successful non-violent protest movement against the British, Reverend King understood that non-violent activism could be the one thing that might break the back of racial discrimination in America. Sadly, it didn't, but the movement led by Dr. King began to erode the power of the vicious discrimination that had held sway in America since the days of slavery. When Americans saw broadcasts of the brutality used against unresisting protesters—both Black and

White—of racial segregation in the south, they were sickened and ashamed. Reverend King's movement forced Americans to look deeply into an ugly mirror, and many, thank God, didn't like what they saw. Although some protesters argued that non-violent activism would never be powerful or sufficient enough to end racial discrimination, Dr. King's work spelled the beginning of the end for legalized segregation, although it could not utterly eradicate the bigotry that still exists in the hearts and minds of some Americans.

This was demonstrated by the length of time it took for all of the United States to adopt Martin Luther King Day, a federal holiday celebrated on the third Monday in January, close to Dr. King's January 15 birthday. Adopted according to the Uniform Monday Holiday Act which fixes certain floating holidays on a particular Monday, Martin Luther King Day was first proposed shortly after his assassination in 1968. It took 15 years before President Ronald Reagan signed the holiday into law in 1983, and another three years before it was first observed on January 20, 1986. It was officially kept for the first time by all 50 states in 2000, nearly 32 years after Dr. King was assassinated. It was not until Senator John McCain of Arizona, a hold-out state against the holiday, made his first presidential bid that he apologized for coming out against the holiday.

It took 32 years for all 50 of these United States to honor the man who only lived 39 years in service to his God and country. Reverend King's sacrifices were monumental, even before he gave his life in the fight against racism. He was raised and ready to enjoy a comfortable, respected life as a minister, taking over from his father, before the Spirit moved him to fight racism. By all accounts, Dr. King would have made a wonderful pastor, and his light could have easily shone for many years on the people in his church and community. Few Christian leaders could have hoped for a better, more useful life. Dr. King himself was torn between the needs of his family, church and community, and the needs of America and the world. In the end, he answered God's call, sacrificing ready-made respectability, his wife and children, his inheritance. In the end, he had a dream, and it was to live in a world much like the one described by Jesus. In the end, Martin Luther King, Jr. gave his living, his vocation, his life for that dream. And America is much better for it.

PRAYER

FATHER, Who cares not for our skin color but for what is in our hearts, help us to honor Your servant, Martin Luther King, Jr., by taking up where he was forced to leave off. Teach us to honor his birthday, an American holiday, not just with words and platitudes, but with works and attitudes. Give us the courage to stand up against racism in our families, schools, workplaces, churches, communities, government. Reverend King wanted to help the United States live up to the promise of equality made by its founders who themselves were merely echoing the teachings of our Lord, Jesus. Give us the strength to do as Dr. King did and take up the cause of racial equality. We pray that we will never be called to make the sacrifices he made; nevertheless, open our hearts to making whatever sacrifices are necessary to continue the peaceful war against racism and inequality wherever we find it. Amen.

ACTIVITY

CONSIDER whether there has ever been a time when you felt or expressed a racist attitude or thought. This is between you and God, so make this an honest examination. Although no one likes to admit such a thought or action, most of us have experienced it. Confess this sin to God. Ask sincerely for forgiveness and for God's help in avoiding such sins in the future. Finally, think of a way you can express repentance, either directly to the person or people you have wronged, or through supporting a group or community fighting racism. Find the strength to follow through on your commitment.

ANNIVERSARY OF BETSY ROSS

WHETHER the image is from some grade school primer or ancient depiction, those of us who are old enough to have learned about Betsy Ross in elementary school tend to envision her as some little, old, grandmother-type. A white-haired lady bent over a length of red, white and blue material, peering down as she carefully sews what we were taught was the first real American flag. It is an indelible image.

The reality is that Betsy Ross lived quite a life up until the moment that our American tradition tells us she took up that needle and thread. She lived through the birth of America and was, in many ways, an emblem of why America came to exist. Her great-grandfather, Andrew Griscom was a Quaker who immigrated in 1680 from England to America where he would be free to practice his religion openly and as he chose. Elizabeth Griscom, later known as Betsy Ross, was the eighth of seventeen siblings born into a Philadelphia Quaker community in 1752 where she lived according to the tenets of faith practiced by the Society of Friends and attended a Quaker school. It was as a child that Betsy learned the skill which would later put her in the history books:

her great-aunt Sarah Elizabeth Ann Griscom taught her how to sew.

Evidently, she was quite good at it because her father apprenticed her to an upholsterer, and it was at this work that she met and fell in love with her first husband, John Ross, the son of an Episcopal assistant rector. The difference in religion caused no little consternation in the Griscom family, and the young couple were forced to elope in 1773 when Betsy was 21. They were married in New Jersey, and as a result, Betsy was expelled from the Quaker community and separated from her family. This religious rift led to one of the most important relationships Betsy would have when the young couple started their own upholstery business and joined Christ Church where they met parishioner George Washington.

Betsy was only 24 years old when her beloved husband joined the local militia and was killed by a gunpowder explosion during the Revolutionary War. Committing herself even more deeply to the War for Independence, she devoted their upholstery business to repairing uniforms and making tents and blankets. She also stuffed paper tube cartridges with musket balls for the Continental Army.

Ross' suffering on behalf of her country was not over. She married her second husband, mariner Joseph Ashburn, in 1777, only to stand by helplessly when his ship was captured by the British in 1780. Ashburn was charged with treason and taken to England where he died in a British prison. Shortly after he was captured, the couple's first daughter, Zilla, died at nine months old, and Betsy was alone when their second child, Eliza, was born. In 1783, Ross married John Claypoole with whom she had five more daughters, but his health was poor and he died in 1817. Nonetheless, Ross carried on with her upholstery business, retiring ten years later. The woman who is renowned for having created the first American flag eventually went completely blind three years before she died in her daughter's home in Philadelphia in 1836.

Some dispute the fact that Ross sewed the first American flag for her old friend, George Washington. Ross' grandson, William J. Canby wrote that she did, indeed, make "with her hands the first flag," and that she presented it to General George Washington when Washington visited Philadelphia in 1776. Whether she did or not will probably never be irrefutably proved, but, in view of Ross' life, it is almost beside the point. Betsy Ross embodied a number of American ideals. First, in her background and her choices, she expressed the concept of religious freedom, a constitutional mainstay which has come to define America in so many ways. Second, she lived the Christian and American notion of community, remaining loyal to God and the people she encountered in her faith, work and married life. Finally, Jesus tells us that we must persevere to the end, and that, Betsy Ross did with a determination and patriotism that combined religious belief and commitment to community/nation in a way that few Americans can match. Enduring tragedy after tragedy, challenge after challenge, Betsy Ross persevered.

PRAYER

SUFFERING Jesus, even in the midst of Your anguish and knowledge about human nature, You urged us to persevere in our faith. Help us to do this, Lord, for it can be so difficult in such troubling times. Just as America struggles to persevere in the righteous ideals which define it, help us to persevere in reflecting Your image and teachings. Let us be true, first and foremost, to You, and also to Your teachings within our families, communities, governments, and nation. Amen.

ACTIVITY

CELEBRATE Betsy Ross' anniversary by persevering. Is there something you've been dreading? Something you haven't found time to do, even though you feel you should? Some challenge that you find difficult and so have shied away from it? Choose something in your life that you have been pushing off to the side, and persevere in doing it. Persevere in praying every day. Persevere in learning to dance. Persevere in trying a new recipe. Persevere in saying a kind word to your grouchy neighbor every morning. Persevere in leaving a better tip for the wait person at your favorite lunch place. Persevere in volunteering.

FEBRUARY 2

GROUNDHOG DAY

Groundhog Day is one of those holidays about which one could easily say, "Only in America!" And yet, not so. The tradition has its foundation in a combination of European agricultural myths and early Christian festivals. It was adopted—and, of course, adapted—in the United States mainly as a reflection of America's European and Christian roots.

Groundhog Day may seem like a slightly goofy tradition today, but the origins were deadly serious. Our ancestors were much more closely tied to nature. Survival, not to mention husbandry and the planting of crops, depended on weather and the length of the seasons. Being able to "predict," or, in the Christian tradition, to pray for, favorable weather was a vital part of life.

There is evidence that Groundhog Day evolved from Candlemas Day, a minor but highly popular holiday kept by early Christians during which clergy blessed and distributed candles to their flocks. The weather that day was thought to be very important and a harbinger of what was to come and what was left of the winter. Historians believe that the Roman legions brought the Candlemas tradition to the German tribes that they conquered. It was the

Germans who first introduced an animal into the scenario, believing that if a certain animal, a hedgehog, appeared on Candlemas Day and saw its shadow because the sun was shining, then there would be six more weeks of winter. This was sometimes referred to as a "second winter," since if winter lasted 12 weeks on the calendar, six weeks represented the half-way mark. It was the hedgehog twist on Candlemas Day that the Germans brought to America.

German immigrants, many settling in Pennsylvania, discovered groundhogs in the region, and because the American groundhog looked something like the hedgehog, the tradition could be continued using the groundhog. Thus, one of the largest and continuing Groundhog Day festivals is based in Punxsutawney, Pennsylvania, where as many as 40,000 people have been known to gather in anticipation of the verdict of Punxsutawney Phil, the nickname of the groundhog in question. The holiday was first celebrated in 1886, and is also popular in New England where agriculture—and the blessed end of winter—is an integral part of life.

Oddly enough, the meaning of the groundhog's shadow has changed from the earliest days of the holiday. Today, some look at it as a good sign if old Phil sees his shadow; they consider that "only" six more weeks of winter is a better alternative than winter lasting well into the end of March or even April.

Not only does Groundhog Day have rather surprising Christian roots, it also embodies another essential Christian concept: hope. Most people look forward to the end of winter, the start of a new season, the return of crops, vegetation, flowers, greenery. In the midst of a dreary, dark winter, sometimes we can begin to believe that Spring and light and fresh food will never be ours again. All we have sometimes is hope. It is the same for Christians. In the midst of dark days and difficult times, we rely on hope: faith in that which is unseen. Punxsutawney Phil is a fun and joyful character, but our hope lies in a much more powerful force: the God Who created the earth and everything in it . . . including hedgehogs and groundhogs.

PRAYER

LORD of all hope and revelry, we thank You for festivals that lift our spirits and help us feel more anchored in our world. Thank You for the hope that comes with laughter and, yes, even silliness. Thank You for each passing day, which in itself, is precious. Thank You for the traditions that remind us that we are part of the earth, part of all of Your creation. Thank

You for ancient customs that come to America from other nations and times, reminding us that we are part of a larger world and have a share in all humanity. Thank You for giving us opportunities to learn from the land and its creatures, and to acknowledge the place they have among us. Amen.

ACTIVITY

PARTICIPATE or check in with one of the Groundhog Day celebrations in the United States. The most noted celebrations take place in Pennsylvania in Punxsutawney, Quarryville, Schuylkill, the Sinnamahoning Valley, and Bucks County. However, many farming or former farming regions offer festivals including a parade in Essex, Connecticut, led by a giant plastic groundhog. If you can't visit or watch a festival, try to find a newspaper story, on-line article, or television report. Are you happy with the groundhog's prediction? Are there ways you can use the remaining days and weeks of winter to become closer to God, more appreciative of His many gifts in creation? As it grows dark, light a candle in recognition of Candlemas Day, the Christian holiday that was the basis for the spread of Groundhog Day from Europe to America. Let your heart and mind and body bask in the light from the candle and the lightheartedness of the festival.

LINCOLN'S BIRTHDAY

ONLY two former Presidents of the United States have birthdays commonly known and observed in the country. Born on February 12, 1809, Abraham Lincoln is the second of them. Recognized as the President who kept the United States united, presided over the Civil War, ended slavery, and was famously assassinated during an evening at the theater by actor and confederate sympathizer, John Wilkes Booth, Lincoln may be the most well-known president ever to serve the American people. Lincoln's birthday was first observed in Buffalo, New York, in 1874.

Despite all this, there is one interesting and little-discussed fact about Lincoln's birthday. Unlike George Washington's birthday, Lincoln's has never been a federal holiday. Some states don't even give him his own holiday, instead recognizing Lincoln on what is officially the federal holiday marking Washington's birthday on Presidents Day, celebrated on the third Monday of February. But Lincoln himself has never had a federal holiday recognizing his extraordinary contributions and achievements.

Perhaps that is because to this day Lincoln, a brilliant orator, remains a somewhat difficult figure in America's history. Many think he surpasses even Washington as the most important, ethical, and plainly decent man who ever served in the office of President. In the "olden" days, before most children were even old enough to attend school, they'd heard about "Honest Abe," who, the story goes, walked miles to return a dime. For these Americans, Lincoln is an icon of honesty and a living representative of the importance of maintaining the *United* States.

Others still see him as the president who interfered with states' rights, wrongly limited the southern states, and sent hundreds of thousands of Americans to their death in the Civil War. While this may be a minority view, the fact that despite repeated Congressional petitions, Lincoln's' birthday has never been made a federal holiday, indicates that a certain number of people still hold it.

How can the same man be, at once, so revered and so despised? Perhaps it is due, once again, to the nature of the massive experiment that is the United States of America. We are a people who live in—and were founded on—a constant state of tension between unity and division. One country, fifty states, and each as determined to maintain and exercise their perceived sovereignty in relation to the federal power as is the nation in relation to other global powers. Not only had some southern states based their economy on slavery, they believed that they had the sovereign right to be slaveholders whether others saw it as right or wrong. For them, the Civil War wasn't just about owning slaves, it was about maintaining the *right* to hold slaves, regardless of what the federal government believed or legislated.

Lincoln believed that all states should adhere to laws based on a certain code of conduct; one that he felt was dictated by the Constitution and the Declaration of Independence. By many accounts, Lincoln prayed and anguished over each death in the Civil War, whether union or confederate. Thousands of books have been written about this issue and about the Civil War, and yet people still disagree. For Christians, Lincoln can also be a troubling figure, but for a different reason. While true Christianity cannot abide slavery or racism, it also cannot approve the kind of war that decimates an entire generation and rends the fabric of a nation. So, what is the verdict on Abraham Lincoln? We may differ on the answer, but fortunately we aren't the ones to make that judgment.

PRAYER

FATHER, in Whom is all freedom and all sovereignty, teach us not to judge others. You have warned us, through scripture and the words of Jesus, against judging, and yet we are tempted again and again to turn our opinions into verdicts. Help us to appreciate that we seldom know all the facts about a person or situation. Teach us that our country is founded on a complicated set of beliefs that defy easy interpretation. Give each of us the insight to recognize what is Your will for us as individuals, and the courage to fulfill it. Keep us from the arrogance which tempts us to decide what is right for others and to judge them according to our perceptions. We praise You for the humanity of Abraham Lincoln and his great achievement of ending slavery and recognizing that a nation founded on freedom could not flourish through enforced servitude. Amen.

ACTIVITY

GO to your local library or bookstore and find a book on Abraham Lincoln. Or, if that is not possible, go on-line and read as much as you can about President Lincoln. If possible, discuss it with one or more friends, acquaintances, or family members. While trying to avoid judgment, ask yourself and/or each other the following questions: Lincoln felt he had no choice but to engage the country in the Civil War—do you agree? Can war, along with its brutality and inevitable loss of life, ever be justified? What was America's Civil War really about? States' rights? Slavery? Racism? Has America ever fully recovered from the Civil War? Do you believe that Americans should have a specific federal holiday recognizing Abraham Lincoln?

FEBRUARY 14

VALENTINE'S DAY

DESPITE all the efforts of serious theologians and religious academics over the years and centuries, Saint Valentine's Day continues to be associated with love, and, to their further dismay, quite often romantic love. The fact that what little we know about the three minor actual Saints Valentine has nothing to do with love, and most certainly nothing to do with romantic love, hasn't prevented people through the ages from firmly connecting Valentine's Day with love. And nowhere is this a more treasured tradition than in America where just about everyone from the smallest school child to her great grandparents exchange some form of Valentine's greeting.

In fact, Saint Valentine's Day has become such a big, loving deal in America that elementary school policies often insist that every child must receive a Valentine card and treat . . . or no child may have one. Anything that resembles or represents love is fair game on Valentine's Day. Some parents make their children heart-shaped pancakes, and some men give their wives heart-shaped diamonds! People choose Valentine's Day to become engaged, marry, forgive each other for tiffs, exchange gifts, bake cakes, buy lavish flower arrangements and expensive chocolates in heart-shaped boxes. In the United States, Valentine's Day rivals Mother's Day for the most flowers and cards purchased and given.

And all because of . . . well, nothing! There were three human Valentines, and according to what evidence we have, none of them seemed to have much to do with love. In fact, they evidently had more to do with death! A number of early Christian martyrs were named Valentine, including the two for whom the day is supposedly celebrated. One was a priest, Valentine of Rome, who was martyred around 270 AD and whose relics are believed to be in churches in both Rome and Ireland. The other was a bishop in Interamna, later called Terni, who is thought to have been martyred around 197 AD during the persecution instituted by the Emperor Aurelian. His relics are in the Basilica of Saint Valentine in Terni. A third, even lesser known Valentine was believed to be martyred in Africa with other Christians.

It was centuries before the three were eventually merged into one tradition when Pope Gelasius I declared February 14 to be Saint Valentine Day in 469, and the holiday became associated with love. In the late Middle Ages, Geoffrey Chaucer was thought to be the first personage to publicly connect the day with romantic love. Probably in an effort—which turned out to be futile—to disassociate the martyrs with an increasingly beloved romantic holiday, in 1969, Pope Paul VI removed Saint Valentine's Day from the official General Roman Calendar of saints. The pope noted that too little was known about the man, or men, called Saint Valentine for him/them to remain on par with more well-known saints.

However, a holiday to love is not something that anyone—or any nation—gives up easily, and America has continued to celebrate Saint Valentine's Day despite the woeful lack of evidence. Indeed, many Christians mark the day worldwide, and perhaps that is a testament to how much we need reminders of love in our religious, and our national, calendars. One thing we do know about the Saints Valentine, after all, is that they died for the love of Jesus Christ, and human love can have no greater model.

PRAYER

JESUS, it was for love of us that You died, and it was for love of You that the earliest martyrs gave their lives. Can death really be a reflection of love, Lord? We honor and praise and, yes, love You for providing us such a model for love. We thank You for the saints and martyrs who reflected that love. We ask You to touch our hearts, minds, and spirits so that the love we feel for each other is transformed into the kind of selfless love You demonstrated for us and that the Saints Valentine showed for You. Teach us to be generous in and with our love. Keep us from the need to ever sacrifice our lives for love, but lead us to give our lives to love. Amen.

ACTIVITY

AT first glance, the Saints Valentine have little to do with the love we've come to associate with them and their day. We might say that the evidence of love is hidden within them and their histories. Consider the people in your life. Is the possibility for love, or to love, hidden somewhere in or among them? Can you find a way to show love to someone who may seem unlovable or unloving or loveless? Can you uncover love in someone or for someone? Could it be offering a kind word? A small gift? Forgetting a slight or an argument? Or, maybe even, sending a Valentine?

WASHINGTON'S BIRTHDAY

MY husband believes that George Washington was our best President, not because he was the first, not because he won the War for Independence, not because he was a general and a leader of men and "The Father of our country," and not even because he won the respect and admiration of a vastly diverse group of people from foot soldiers to founding fathers. No, my husband elevates Washington to the number one position because he was reluctant to serve.

With all of Washington's stellar accomplishments, this reluctance is what sets him apart from just about everyone who came after him. And his reluctance was not simply about serving as President. After winning the War for Independence, Washington deliberately resigned from being general, wanting to ensure that the fledgling democracy would not move back into a direction of dictatorship. He retired to his home, Mount Vernon, and only returned to public life to oversee the drafting of the constitution during the Constitutional Convention in 1787. After being elected to one term as President, Washington again wanted to retire but was unanimously supported in the electoral college for a second term.

Evidence abounds of Washington's humility and concern about maintaining the United States of America as a republic of and by the people. When offered a royal crown, he hastily refused any such trappings that would remind people of the British colonizers they'd recently defeated. Washington also fought against sectarianism and political parties, refusing to join a particular political party when members of his cabinet, Alexander Hamilton and Thomas Jefferson, founded opposing nascent parties.

Exhausted after almost a lifetime of protecting, serving, and trying to establish our nation, Washington flatly turned down a third term in office, establishing a precedent for the two-term limit we have on the Presidency today. He was also determined not to die in office, believing that such a situation would set an undesirable precedent and once again evoke the British monarchy. In every move he made as President, Washington was careful to embody prudence, balance, honesty, and a willingness to put the newborn country and its people before his own needs and ego. In his now famous "Farewell Address," Washington warned his countrymen against partisanship, sectionalism, and interfering in foreign wars.

So, what happened? It seems we live in a time now when candidates for political office much less important that the Presidency will do everything to win including buy it outright; and they don't do that only because it's illegal. How did we, as a nation, move from the high ground established by Washington to the partisanship, vicious tactics, and money-burning elective process we now have?

Possibly, we and our leaders have forgotten what George Washington seemed to know so well: that power can easily corrupt the best of us. That's why he walked away from it so often. Most people seeking to govern in America may well have the best of intentions at the outset. But, like so many of the leading figures in the Bible, temptations abound. It is so easy to believe we are right when everyone around us is supporting our opinion and money is pouring in and the competition is fierce. From there, it's a sly, small step to thinking everything we do to gain power is OK because we would do such a good job that we *should* have power. We *deserve* power. And then another downward step brings us to attacking anyone who would oppose us.

If this is an ugly picture to us, imagine what it looks like to God. Yet before we heap too much disdain upon our politicians and elected officeholders, maybe we should do as Jesus said, and take a long look at the log in our own eye. How often do we seek power in a relationship or community or church group, convinced that we will do the right thing, that we have everyone's best interest at heart? How seldom do we do what Washington did and reject an offer of power and prestige? How closely do we examine our consciences the way we expect our politicians to examine theirs? Perhaps if we did more of this, and if they did more of this, America could stay the course to greatness that Washington put us on.

PRAYER

KING of kings and Lord of lords, teach us as individuals to examine our motives when we seek control or power in any situation. In all that we do, keep us within the bounds of Christianity so that we may act with humility and according to Your will. Help us to choose leaders who are thoughtful, honest, and without rancor. Lead us, Lord, to the higher ground on which America was founded. Amen.

ACTIVITY

CONSIDER a relationship, situation, or group in which you've held power. Examine your actions and motives. Why did you want this position of power? How did you attain it? How have you acted toward others when you were the strongest? What have you done—or what are you willing to do—to maintain your advantage? Answer these questions honestly and then ask yourself one more: what would George Washington have done?

MARCH—SECOND SUNDAY

DAYLIGHT SAVINGS TIME BEGINS

THIS is the day that many Americans long for. It's not an official holiday, secular or religious. There are no presents. No one will slave over a hot stove all day long, working to prepare a huge, celebratory meal. There will be no elaborate toasts. Nonetheless, the day we "turn the clocks ahead"; or, as we were all taught to remember, "Spring Ahead, Fall Back," is a red-letter day for many Americans.

It can mean many things. Most importantly, in this country it means that we seem to have more daylight. The truth is we don't really get another second of daylight by "springing ahead." What we get, however, is an hour more of light at the end of the day, and, boy, do we welcome it at this point in the year. It almost doesn't matter that the dawn comes an hour later; it's the encroaching darkness of nightfall that many of us want to postpone, and today, we get to do just that.

Growing up in my home, daylight savings time weekend was a major event. My parents both worked, and by the time they got home in the evening during winter, it was all but dark. There was nothing to be done but get supper on the table and hope for a decent basketball game on the television afterwards. Then, suddenly, with the turn of a wrist or a key, depending upon the clock in question, all that changed. No more swiftly approaching nights. No more rushing right into the house at the end of the workday. No more postponing any yard or garage work until the weekend. My father, who enjoyed his yard and a good walk or bike ride almost as much as he craved the light, would be super-charged on the weekend that "the time changed." In fact, by the time the rest of us got up on Saturday morning, all the clocks were likely to be changed. We had to be careful to go to church on Saturday evening an hour before the clocks in our house dictated.

It almost seems like a miracle every year when daylight savings time comes around. Long days of school and work no longer end in near-darkness. Kids can get in a little outdoor time before dinner and homework and the Internet or T.V. Adults who have been commuting to work in the murky morning and returning home in the dusk get to see the sun and to feel, hopefully, a little more warmth. To some more analytical minds, the thrill of daylight savings time seems a little foolish. After all, nothing really changes in terms of the length of light apportioned over every 24 hours.

But for those of us who welcome the sunlight as a reflection of the light of God, daylight savings time is surely a small miracle. It mirrors the larger miracle of light as a symbol of God-with-us. We know that God made the sun and the moon and the stars to illuminate the world for us. We know that Moses, having seen God, became so blindingly bright himself that the Israelites could not look directly upon him. We know Jesus as the light of the world. We know that His birth was marked by a blazing star. We know that His transfiguration was too bright for the apostles to gaze upon. We know the Holy Spirit came in the form of tongues of fire. We know that we are to let our own God-given light shine upon all people.

We know that we do not want to be "a people who walk in darkness." Today, God blesses us with a reminder that we are not.

PRAYER

JESUS, Light of the world, Beacon for this country, illuminate our way. On this first day of Daylight Savings Time, remind us to shine with the light of the Gospels and to reveal Your teachings in the way we conduct ourselves. When our lives and our nation seem to be overcome with darkness, show us the path back to You. Help our leaders to seek to exchange the harsh glare of gunfire and explosives for the glow of understanding and generosity. Teach us and our countrymen and women to shine, not with the dull sheen of gold, but with the glorious glow of the Golden Rule. Lead us to use this "extra" hour of light at the end of the day to rejoice in Your light and to do Your will. Amen.

ACTIVITY

THIS evening, take note of the "new" light. Even if the weather is not perfect, spend that last hour of daylight deliberately and thoughtfully. Put away your cell-phone, i-phone, and computer. Go outside if you can, and if you can't, take the time to look out a window or door. If possible, watch the sun set. Open a window if it's not too cold, even if just for a few moments. Breathe in God's gift of glowing, evening air. Delay turning on lights (and the television!) in your house or workplace and choose to use God's natural light for as long as possible. Have dinner by the light of the evening and perhaps a candle or two. Praise God for the gift of this light.

HARRIET TUBMAN'S ANNIVERSARY

IT'S difficult to celebrate Harriet Tubman's birthday because no one is sure precisely when it was. Such was the life of slavery that Tubman was born into: a slave was not even considered important enough—human enough—to possess a birth-day. It was this stripping of humanity and dignity that Tubman spent her entire life fighting. In that lifelong battle, she served as a slave, abolitionist, humanitarian, Union spy during the Civil War, and women's rights advocate.

A committed Christian in both word and deed, Tubman was called "Moses" because she led her people out of slavery. Believed to have been born in 1822, she was raised in slavery in Maryland and frequently beaten by her owners. As a child she suffered a severe head wound while enslaved, and as a result for the rest of her life, Tubman suffered with seizures, narcolepsy, headaches, and other disabilities. She also experienced visions and extraordinary dreams which she came to believe were revelations from God. So in addition to her many other roles in life, Harriet Tubman was also a Christian mystic. And it may have been these mystic experiences which led her to boldly live Jesus' words, "The truth will set you free."

While in her twenties, Harriet Tubman escaped from the last of a series of slave-holders, fleeing to Philadelphia. But it was not enough for her to be free when others were still prisoners. Despite the great risk of recapture or even death, she returned to Maryland, determined to free her family. Slowly, small group by small group, she took her relatives out of Maryland and toward freedom. Still, Tubman was not satisfied. Using the Underground Railroad, a system of abolitionist activists and safe houses for runaway slaves, Tubman, who was then doing the work of a modern-day Moses, returned to the South over a dozen times, eventually leading over 70 people to freedom. Always traveling by night, Tubman was known for never losing a slave entrusted to her care.

When the United States Congress passed the ill-advised Fugitive Slave Law of 1850, which made it illegal to help runaway slaves anywhere in the United States and required even abolitionist states to assist in the capture and return of runaways, Tubman began ferrying her passengers even farther north into Canada where slavery was illegal.

Still, Harriet Tubman did not rest. After the outbreak of the Civil War, she worked for the Union army, again taking on many roles including cook, nurse, armed scout, and finally spy. She became an extremely valued member of the army, eventually becoming the first woman in the country to lead an armed division when she guided Union soldiers in the Combahee River Raid, which freed over 700 slaves in South Carolina.

Tubman, who ended up living for nearly a century, spent the post-war years with her family in Auburn, New York, caring for her parents and continuing to work for freedom and dignity. She joined the women's suffrage movement and founded a home for elderly African Americans, where she later spent the end of her life. She died in 1922, having lived long enough to see the Nineteenth Amendment, prohibiting any United States citizen from being denied the right to vote based on gender, ratified by Congress in 1920.

It is no surprise that Harriet Tubman was a devout Christian and that she was blessed with visions and dreams from God. She gave her entire life to the pursuit of freedom and dignity for all people, the Christian ideal. In so doing, she helped shape and promote that ideal as a concept intrinsic to the American experience.

PRAYER

ONE of the most striking things about Harriet Tubman is actually something we don't know: where was her anger? With all the horrors she was made to suffer, all the human carnage and despair she must have witnessed, all the glaring inequality that she experienced, she never let anger cripple her or drag her down or keep her from her objective of freedom and dignity for all. Father, protect us from rage and despair. Keep us focused on doing Your work so that we are not consumed by anger, even righteous anger at injustices and bigotry. Help us to avoid the paralyzing and destructive force of useless anger. When we do experience anger, let it be the fuel that fires us to do good and take risks on behalf of others. Amen.

ACTIVITY

IS there something you are angry about, or have been angry about recently? Consider your feelings and actions. Is it your impulse to react to your anger and hurt by lashing out or even seeking punishment or vengeance? That would be part of human nature. But instead, seek within yourself for that Divine Spark that glowed so brightly in Harriet Tubman. Think of a way you can use your anger to do something positive. It may be as simple as forgiving or praying for the person you are angry with. It may be something monumental like standing up for freedom and equality in a public forum. Whatever it is, work to transform your anger into a good action.

SAINT PATRICK'S DAY

WE hear it at least once every year around this time: "Everyone's Irish on Saint Patrick's Day!" Except, of course, the Saint himself. Patrick was probably born in or near Rome around 389 AD, the son of a Roman deacon named Calpurnius. Patrick was well-schooled in the Roman Catholic faith by the time he was kidnapped and carried away captive to Ireland, at about the age of 16, where he was forced into service as a herdsman, a life that was decidedly much harsher than that he'd enjoyed in the Roman Empire. Ireland had not been converted, and Patrick is thought to have suffered greatly because of the paganism he encountered there, although he later came to believe that his experience made his faith and prayer/contemplative life stronger.

Although he escaped after six years of enforced servitude and returned home, the young Christian was unable to put Ireland behind him. He felt that God wanted him to return and convert the island nation, and his dreams confirmed this belief. Patrick began to study at the monastery of Lerins to prepare for this mission and was ordained about 417. However, Patrick's superiors were not as con-

vinced as he that his future was in Ireland, and
they did not grant him permission to return
until 431, nearly 20 years after he escaped.
When the bishop he had been sent to help died
shortly after Patrick's return, Patrick was made
bishop. His work began in earnest then, and
Patrick traveled tirelessly to every corner of the
island in his mission to convert the Irish people
to Christianity. Despite efforts by the Druids to
prevent his work, Patrick was successful, even
converting members of Ireland's ruling clan.

In 442, Pope Leo called Patrick back to
Rome where the Pope recognized his success
by commissioning him to establish the Church
of Ireland. Encouraged, Patrick returned to
Ireland and began to organize the island by
appointing bishops in various communities
throughout the country. Building upon the
deeply mystical, spiritual vein that flowed
through the people of Ireland, Patrick was able
to establish monasteries and places of learning
that rivaled any in what was then continental
Europe. His success was so complete that it
was eventually Irish monks who converted
parts of England, France, and Switzerland to
Christianity. Saint Patrick died on March 17,
461, after having completed *Confessions*, his
life's literary effort which gave Christians even
greater insight to his work and faith.

So, everyone being Irish on Saint Patrick's Day is about a lot more than green beer! Patrick's journey from slave-worker to the spiritual father of Ireland was so astonishing that many people believe to this day that he was Irish. The fact that Ireland came to be perceived as one of the "most Catholic" countries on earth is also a testament to Patrick's achievement.

And it did not stop with Ireland—or even England, France and Switzerland. When Irish citizens began to immigrate to America, they brought their religion with them. Their faith and traditions were so strong that they took root in what had been primarily a Protestant nation. The Irish immigrants labored hard, established beachheads in many urban communities, and built churches. Although discrimination against them was initially fierce, in short order, they began to rise in politics as well as in church life. Today, Irish-Americans are so well-established that they are part and parcel of every aspect of American life, even to the point where, indeed, "Everyone is Irish on Saint Patrick's Day."

PRAYER

LORD, it is so true that You work in mysterious ways! Surely, the young Roman who was stolen from his home and country over 1,600 years ago could not have imagined You would guide him through that ordeal and return him to the place where he was so harshly treated. And yet in doing so, You strengthened Christianity so powerfully that it spread over continents and across oceans. Father, we praise You for sending Your Spirit out into the world and upon women and men like Saint Patrick. We worship You for Your wisdom and generosity to we, Your people. We thank You for the positive influence on America of Saint Patrick and the Irish Christians who came to identify so completely with him and his work. Amen.

ACTIVITY

HONOR Saint Patrick and the Irish in America today by doing something besides drinking green beer or Irish whiskey! Attend church and give thanks for the Saint's faith and his consequent positive influence. Read *St. Patrick: His Confession and Other Works* by Father Neil O'Donoghue (Catholic Book Publishing, Corp.). Learn something about Irish culture, Irish mystics, and the great monasteries that Patrick helped found. Study the history of the Irish in America and note their determination and widespread achievements.

FIRST DAY OF SPRING

THE first day of Spring, otherwise known as the vernal equinox, may be one of the oldest festival days in the world. For as long as we humans have been aware of our surroundings, we have been profoundly cognizant of the seasons. Not so long ago, people lived and died according to what the seasons wrought, and in some areas of the world they still do. It is no wonder that the coming of Spring is so widely heralded in America and throughout the world.

It has been this way for millennia. Spring has always meant a return to life and light and food for humankind. The first humans, we imagine, must have felt a sense of hope and renewal, not to mention a practical knowledge that with the warmth and light and longer days would also come new plant and animal life. In other words, they'd have more food and medicine, clothing and tents. Spring has always meant survival.

Ancient societies took note of Spring-time, even changing the lengths of the "hours" of the day, so that they would be longer during Spring and Summer than during Winter. By the Roman Water Clocks, time was a celebration of the gentler seasons: the third hour of the day, about 9 a.m. by modern standards, lasted 44 minutes on the first day of Winter, but 75 minutes on the first day of Summer. Humans have always craved spiritual and physical renewal, and thus have reveled in the sun and warmth that start to strengthen on the first day of Spring.

Because it is in the Northern Hemisphere, America's vernal equinox represents the first day of Spring; however, in the Southern Hemisphere, today marks the first day of Autumn, or the autumnal equinox. It is interesting to think that while we celebrate the beginning of new life, more sun and new crops, the people in South America, Southern Africa, Australia and other parts of the south begin their season of moribund life and shadows. Regardless of hemisphere, the entire world experiences the equinox as a 24-hour period where day and night are roughly equal, about 12 hours each, because the sun has taken its twice annual position directly over the Earth's equator.

Although we who are weary of winter tend to think of the first day of Spring in terms of daylight, the actual translation of equinox is "equal night." This is an interesting contrast for Christians because it reminds us that even the best and most joyful days of our lives are followed by night; and just as important, the darkest and saddest nights are followed by bright days. When we are in the midst of such times, we often forget that we are in a cycle that is perfectly balanced by God. We do not always feel that. We may feel that the dark, difficult times will never end; and similarly, when we rejoice, we don't like to remember that pain may be just around the corner. Just as God is the Guide for the seasons, so it is with us. We must put our faith in Him to balance out the seasons of our lives, and we must be prepared for whatever He sends, knowing that His plan is better than ours, even when it seems incomprehensible.

Nature does not question her Creator, and her seasons come and go in due time. Can we not be faithful in the same way?

PRAYER

GOD of all seasons, thank You for the gift of the first day of Spring! We rejoice in the new life all around us, even if it is still buried under the snow and ice! We praise You for every sign—from the smallest purple crocus to the brave robin—that the earth is once again renewing itself. We are in awe of You, O Lord, for putting the sun precisely where it belongs at this moment on this day, again. We are humbled by Your majesty, which turns nature to Your will and gives us all that we need in due season. Keep us always aware of Your Presence through the glory of nature, and keep us always grateful for Your renewal of our spirits and our bodies and of all that is around us. Amen.

ACTIVITY

TODAY, search for a sign of Spring. Look for a crocus or the tip of a daffodil or hyacinth, maybe peeking through a crust of snow. Cut some forsythia and bring them in to your home to start "forcing" the blossoms. Notice the brightness of the sun. Search for a newly turned patch of soil for an early garden. Take note of where snow and ice has melted, even if just a little. Hunt for a robin. If you live in the south or west, go to the store and buy fruit or flowers that you associate with Spring. And if you're sitting in North Dakota watching the snow fly and the gray sky turn pewter, open a gardening catalogue and order some seeds. Spring really does begin today!

ANNUNCIATION OF THE LORD

THOUGH it is not yet Easter, for Christians today is the official start of the Christmas season! Technically speaking, that is. This is the day that is precisely nine months before the Birthday of Jesus, otherwise known as Christmas. Therefore we celebrate March 25 as the day that the angel, Gabriel, announced to the young virgin, Mary, that she would bear the Son of God, the Savior of the world, *into* the world. It is obviously a momentous day, and there has probably been almost as much art created depicting the miraculous event we honor today as there has been of the Nativity itself.

And yet, it can seem strange that this Holy day occurs in the midst of Lent, a season of repentance for Christians, a season of suffering. During some years, the Annunciation takes place during Holy Week, the most solemn week in the Christian calendar. But we can't really schedule these things, can we? We can't really decide that we will suffer this week and rejoice the next. We can't say that next month will be a month of joy, undimmed by even the smallest sorrow; nor can we say that during the month after that we will experience anguish, untouched by the smallest smile or sign of hope. We don't have that kind of power.

In the timing of the Annunciation—both today and in history—we see that only God has that kind of power. For Christians today, the Annunciation is a glimmer of hope during a season of sorrow. It comes as a reminder that the One Whose agony we suffer over now is also the One Whose birth we will joyfully celebrate before the year is out. In the same way, the Annunciation came to Mary at a time of uncertainty and political unrest. The Jewish people were under the occupying legions of Rome. They were burdened by Roman law and Roman taxes, and disgusted by Roman pagan worship. Jewish rebels were being summarily tortured and crucified. There was little in the way of hope for a happy ending.

But that was the time that God chose to send Gabriel to Mary. And suddenly, in the midst of seemingly endless suffering: hope!

God's relationship with humankind is one of constant renewal. He is forever—literally—providing us with joy in the midst of sorrow and opportunities to repent in the midst of joy. God renews us daily, moment-to-moment!, not only in our annual calendar of holidays.

Just as the Israelites were bowed in grief and anger under the Roman occupation at the time of the Annunciation, so the United States struggles today with many seemingly unresolvable problems. Many of us feel besieged, not by the Roman army, but by challenges and difficulties that can seem as devastating. We face terrorism on a global scale, poverty in America, homelessness, hunger, unemployment, environmental crises, rising competition from nations like China, hatred, divisiveness in our government, and many other distressing problems. It would surely be easy for Americans to sink into a morass of gloom and depression where no sign of hope or light can shine through.

But today we celebrate the Annunciation. What good news is God offering to each of us right now? To America?

PRAYER

FATHER, today we remember the day that You sent Gabriel to Mary, to the Israelites, to bring them a sign of light in the midst of darkness. Thank You for that miracle, both for what it meant to the world then and now, and what it signifies to us today. Lord, You alone know the suffering of Your people, of this nation today. Remind us to search for the light of hope. Teach us to keep our eyes open in readiness for Your words of joy. Send us miracles, large and small, to guide us through the darkness onto the path You set aside for us,

Lord. And let us be like Mary, ready to accept and honor Your call.

ACTIVITY

SEARCH for light in the midst of any darkness you may be experiencing in your life, and look for signs of hope amid the challenges faced by America. God's glimmers of light are there, but often you must look for—and be open to—them. For you personally, it may be something as small as a warm, sunny day in the middle of March, or as large as a good lead on a new or better job. Did your troubled child give you a small smile or a friendly word? Did you receive a flier with a coupon for something you need or have been meaning to buy? Did someone you've been feuding with at home or work give it a rest today? Did you watch a small bird enjoy the seeds you put out? Have you lost a few pounds or started to control your blood pressure, diabetes, cholesterol? As for America, can you find a newspaper or on-line article with some good news? Can you find a story or news report on organizations in the United States working to protect the environment, develop clean energy, help the homeless, feed the starving people in Africa, support the peace process in the Middle East, train the unemployed? Annunciations are all around you, if only you look for them.

EASTER

TODAY is the absolute pinnacle of the Global Christian calendar: the day that defines life for Christians all over the world. It is the day we celebrate the Resurrection of Jesus Christ, the event that actually stopped and then restarted history; the moment when a precious heart and breath that had been stopped, began again.

And yet, in America (and other western nations), Easter seems to be given less and less attention. Increasingly, it is eclipsed by what people perceive to be the more festive (read: commercially active) season of Christmas. When is the last time you heard a parent say they were buying an "Easter outfit" for their child or children, or even themselves, to wear to church? When is the last time any of the major television stations ran repeats of *The Greatest Story Ever Told* or *The Robe* all Easter morning or afternoon? Can you imagine those wonderful old movies being given precedence by the networks over the Sunday interview and talk-news shows? How often do families color hard-boiled eggs, with the adults explaining how the egg represents the Resurrection? When have you or someone you know last attended a sunrise Easter service?

Of course that doesn't mean that Americans don't recognize Easter. However, too often these days that recognition takes the form of an expensive brunch, a lavish dinner, a hand-woven basketful of chocolate, the Easter bunny, stuffed animals, and anything that is pastel colored. Nothing is wrong with all that, as long as everyone is aware of the reason for these special treats: Jesus is risen! Allelujiah!

Is His Resurrection the foundation of our Easter celebrations? In these times of fierce competition between the world's most powerful nations for control of money, land, weapons, resources, intelligence, the media, and the very hearts and souls of people, are we fully aware of what this day meant in history and still means today? Do we understand that this is the day that marked God's triumph over sin and death? A power greater than anything man had, or has since, produced was unleashed on that day. *This* day. So, Americans: lift your faces from your elegant plates, put down the champagne flutes, don't unwrap another chocolate, turn off the Sunday politicians, drag the kids away from the computer games. And remember that this is the day the Lord has made. Rejoice in it, and be glad, experiencing full well its true meaning.

PRAYER

R ISEN Jesus, remind us of the pure, divine power of this holy day. Capture our attention, Lord! Help us to remember that this is no ordinary holiday, but the most powerful of holy days. Turn us back to You and fill us with the strength of Your Spirit. Lead us to rejoice with full hearts and minds in the celebration of Your Resurrection. Fill us with a dawning comprehension of the impact of Your life, death, and rising. Let this day be a reminder for America, as well, Lord; a reminder that all things: nations, politics, governments, human power must all eventually bow to Your will. Let us do so with humble hearts and grateful minds. Amen.

ACTIVITY

D O something this Easter weekend that will give the glorious meaning of Easter proper recognition. Return to a custom you may have observed as a child, or create a new tradition. Decorate Easter eggs with your family or a group that includes children while talking about the spiritual symbolism of the egg. Rent a faith-based Easter movie and watch it alone or with others. Help prepare your church for the various services. Host or join a family or community meal where everyone talks in turn about what Easter means to them. Discuss the ways in which Easter is celebrated in America. Read the Resurrection Gospels to yourself or others; and if you are alone, write down how it makes you feel; if you are in a gathering, talk about these feelings. Bring a bouquet of Easter flowers to a friend, relative, or even a stranger who is in a hospital or otherwise confined.

APRIL 1

APRIL FOOL'S DAY

APRIL Fool's Day is not a purely American festival. It is actually, and rather surprisingly, more of a global celebration. In a number of countries, including the United Kingdom, Cyprus, and South Africa, the traditions are a little different with jokes only allowed before noon with anyone committing a hoax after noon called an "April Fool." In the United States and the majority of other nations, including France, Italy, South Korea, Japan, Russia, The Netherlands, Germany, Brazil, Canada, Ireland, and Australia, the joking and hoaxing is an all-day affair.

Although not an official national holiday in the United States, April Fool's Day is a cherished festival of, well, foolishness. It is a day for pranks and practical jokes, jests and tricks. Otherwise august daily newspapers run bizarre stories or fake headlines. Teachers may find fake spiders—or worse fake things—on their desks. Siblings and friends try to outwit each other. Office colleagues scheme and plot.

My mother and I used to go to great lengths to try to "fool" one another. You would think that after so many years it would be impossible; that both of us would be on our guard every minute of every first day of April. But we've devised elaborate scenarios that some-times involve other people to make the "trick" easier to pull off. Once I called her and told her I'd had my very long (at the time) hair cut very short. She sneered, "Yeah, sure, and it just so happens to be April Fool's Day, right?" The best part was that I *had* had it cut, deliberately that day after years of letting it grow, just to pull one over on her.

From the number of countries that celebrate April Fool's Day, it is clear that the need for laughter and levity transcends borders and cultures, not to mention the East-West and North-South divide. Most agree that the first mention of April Foolery and the date, April First, was in Chaucer's Canterbury Tales, writ-ten in 1392. How and why it "went viral" as we say these days is anybody's guess. Mine would be simply that we all need a little fun. I don't think it's a coincidence that April Fool's Day falls at the very beginning of Spring when our spirits cry out for the chance to express a little joy, to be a little wild, to raise our faces to the bright sky and smile.

America, too, needs to smile and laugh and joke a bit. We are, if nothing else, a serious nation. We study every trend, scrutinize every on-line article, follow every bit of health news, attend to bloggers and 24-hour news shows.

We analyze ourselves, our families, our spouses, our religions, our country, our politicians. We even make recreation serious, planning vacations and days off until the plans are more important than the time and space. April Fool's Day gives us an opportunity to blow off steam, to be frivolous and silly. And it is comforting that nations and cultures all over the world take advantage of this festival to do the same. Nationally and globally, we live in serious, difficult times; and putting aside a day for goofing around, from Russia to Japan to Brazil to the United States, is a blessing.

It could very well be a greater blessing than we know, something more than just a few laughs. April Fool's Day is a reminder of how short human life is in the eternity that is God. We take ourselves so seriously. God must smile at our self-important actions and antics. We tend to forget, in our striving and competing and analyzing, how limited we are and how tiny and ineffectual in the huge span of time allotted humankind on the earth. We are all fools before the One who made time and space. So, why not enjoy it once in a while?

PRAYER

SPIRIT of laughter and joy, infect us with the revelry and rejoicing that comes to those who know they live in God's presence. Help us to see the laughter and light in our lives. Remind us to cheer those around us whenever we can and to smile at our own seriousness. Give us the perspective to know that, in Your great scheme of things, we live this life in a mere moment, and that some of that moment should be spent lighthearted in the confidence that You are smiling at and with us. Teach us to go to great lengths to make another smile. Let us be the foolish tools of Your great wisdom and love and forgiveness. Amen.

ACTIVITY

MAKE at least one person (though the more, the merrier) smile or, better yet, chuckle or laugh, today. Tell a good joke. Recount an amusing internet anecdote. Play a good-natured prank. Buy a colleague a cup of coffee. Read a funny article or story aloud to someone. Make a face. Wear something fun or unusual. Tickle your child. Talk nonsense to her. Play a game with him. Call your spouse by a silly endearment. Every time you make someone smile, thank God for the blessing.

APRIL 15
TAX DAY

AMERICA has a long and checkered history when it comes to taxes. Ostensibly, taxes are what started the American Revolution. The American colonists grew tired of paying levies to England, particularly because the American colony had no representation in the British parliament. Hence, the outraged cry of "No taxation without representation," which echoed as passionately nearly 250 years ago during the Tea Party, which saw colonists dump tea exported from England into the Boston Harbor rather than pay taxes on it, as it does today, among members of the new Tea Party. Is it true that if the American colonists had representatives in the British Parliament, then they would not have revolted against their "mother" country? Who can say? The colonists' list of grievances by the time they began dumping tea in Boston was probably already too long to prevent the War for Independence.

Throughout its history, America has always been leery of taxes. In the early years, right after the Revolution, the Founding Fathers well knew that they didn't dare impose too many taxes on a population that equated taxation with tyranny. A Federal Income Tax was not fully established until the Revenue Act of 1861, and then only to help fund the Civil War. Tax day then was June 30, but before long the Commissioner of Internal Revenue is believed to have argued for an earlier date. History suggests that many of the wealthiest American residents, who in those days paid the lion's share of the income tax, vacationed during the summer, making it more difficult to collect the June 30 tax.

There have been many challenges to the income tax in America, and we're not just talking about Willie Nelson! In some cases these challenges were supported by the Supreme Court as in Pollock v. Farmers Loan & Trust in 1895 which challenged the Wilson-Gorman Tariff Act of 1894, taxing incomes over $4,000. The Supreme Court effectively ruled against the government, saying that the unapportioned taxes on interest, dividends, and rents were actually direct taxes and therefore violated the Constitution's rule that direct taxes must be apportioned. Of course, necessity is the mother of invention, and so 18 years later, a government in need of money managed to get the Sixteenth Amendment ratified, thus giving the United States Congress the authority to tax all income regardless of previous rules about apportionment.

The federal individual income tax filing deadline at that time, in 1913, was March 1, perhaps to prevent those sneaky vacationers from slipping out of town. In 1918, the filing deadline was changed to March 18, and in 1955, it was moved again to today's date, April 15. If that date falls on a Saturday, Sunday, or holiday, the filing date moves to the first day that is not a Saturday, Sunday, or holiday. But in a country made up of devoutly independent states—and people—who don't much like taxes anyway, even this date isn't inviolable. When Tax Day fell on Patriot's Day, a civic holiday in Massachusetts and Maine, the federal tax deadline used to be extended for taxpayers— not just in Maine and Massachusetts, but also in Maryland, New Hampshire, New York, Vermont, and Washington D.C., because the Internal Revenue Service Processing Center for those states was in Massachusetts and the unionized federal employees had a contractual day off.

But in the end, we all know the old saying: The only two things we can't avoid are death and taxes. And most Americans today dislike paying taxes almost as much . . . well, OK, not as much as dying. However, paying taxes is not only the price for the privilege of living in this country, it is, more importantly, a deeply

Christian action. In America, the money raised from taxes funds a myriad of programs that are in keeping with Jesus' command to love one another. Our taxes pay for food, housing, and medical care for the very poor, not to mention our neighbors, parents, and the elderly. Taxes pay municipal employees who keep us safe, teachers who educate and help raise our children, soldiers who protect us, and the list goes on. The taxes we pay reflect Jesus' tenet to love your neighbor as yourself, because they support and improve both our lives and the lives of others.

PRAYER

LORD, I can hide nothing from You. You know that I am not thrilled about paying my taxes. Remind me that in doing so, I am helping to do Your work. I am helping to care for others and for myself. Help me to understand that the democracy and the decency upon which America is founded depends upon the goodness of her citizens. Thank You for making me one of them. Forgive me for the times I feel selfish and unwilling to do my part.

ACTIVITY

TODAY, and for the next few days, keep taxes in the back of your mind. Not in the resentful way they may normally reside in your brain, but instead, seek to observe all the ways in which your tax money contributes to the good of your neighbors, your community, your country, and yourself. When you hear a fire siren or pass a school bus; if you see a senior citizen (or are one!) or a young mother reliant on food stamps; if you hear of someone getting a loan or grant for college or job training; when you buy food from your grocer confident that it is safe and fresh . . . all of these things and so many more can serve as helpful reminders of the Christianity inherent in paying taxes.

EARTH DAY

THERE is a small but intense and growing movement in the United States to associate Christianity with environmentalism. The bond grows from a deeply held belief that God created the earth and made humankind her stewards, and that therefore, as children of God charged with caring for His gift of the earth and nature, we must properly support and respect our environment. Interestingly, this movement encompasses both passionate liberal Christians and fundamentalist Christians who find their motivation for faith-based environmentalism in scripture.

The origins of Earth Day, which was first established in America, incorporate this Christian perspective. Some claim that the notion of Earth Day was initially conceived by a man named John McConnel in 1969 during a United Nations Educational, Scientific and Cultural Organization (UNESCO) conference in San Francisco. Regardless of who first thought up the day, the first proclamation of an Earth Day was issued in San Francisco; and it was not lost on Christians, especially Catholics, that San Francisco was named after Saint Francis, the patron saint of ecology.

The first actual Earth Day was celebrated in San Francisco and a few other major cities on March 21, 1970. The first day of Spring was approved as the official Earth Day by the United Nations, and was celebrated thereafter internationally.

Another Earth Day, also originating in America in the same time frame, was instituted by the United States Senator, Gaylord Nelson, and this "second" first Earth Day was held on April 22, 1970 as an environmental education day. It was observed with an increasing number of events and programs in America over the next 20 years and eventually "went international" in 1990 when Earth Day programs were observed in over 140 countries. The environmental holiday has continued to grow. Currently, Earth Day is celebrated in over 175 countries, many of which have stretched the event into a week-long ecological festival, highlighting education, preservation, clean energy, smart development, and other related innovations. The worldwide celebration has grown so large that the programs and events are overseen globally by the Earth Day Network. Although the United Nations originally sanctioned March 21 as its authorized Earth Day, in 2009 it proclaimed April 22 to be International Mother Earth Day.

The evolution of Earth Day over the past four decades represents a meeting of the secular and the spiritual in its focus on nature. From a secular perspective, every nation in the world, and most especially the United States, has a stake in preserving and protecting the earth and its resources, and many suggest that we may have already pushed Mother Nature too far. Without national and comprehensive global environmental policies, no government—and no amount of governing—will make up for what we are losing. From a physical and wholly practical point-of-view, humankind cannot survive without the provisions of the earth. Nor can we escape our spiritual ties to, and responsibility for, the creation that God provided for us. Many of us are just starting to understand that by giving us "dominion" over the earth and all its creatures, God was not giving us leave to destroy and deplete at will. For all Christians and all Americans, "dominion" in this case must mean stewardship, and Earth Day is a reminder that the sooner we get started with that, the better.

PRAYER

ALMIGHTY Creator, in giving humankind dominion over the earth, You charged us with care for all Your creation. Thank You for giving us the pragmatic and programmatic reminder that Earth Day provides us. Forgive us for the times we have fallen prey to greed, gluttony, and self-absorption in the pursuit of our own needs over the needs of the environment You created for us. Teach us how to care for Your creation, Lord, and how to plan with an eye toward the future of all people. Heal the wounds that we have made to the earth, Lord, as only You can. Let our stewardship never be weakened by pettiness, divisiveness, or ego-driven competition as we seek to do what's best for Your precious gift of the earth. Amen.

ACTIVITY

DO something today and this week to honor God by helping the environment. The list is endless. Use less electricity. Plant a sapling. Start a vegetable garden. Attend an Earth Day program. Read a book on environmentalism. Look into having your home made more energy efficient through an energy audit, possibly with your local utility company. Buy twisty light bulbs. Start a discussion. Join a discussion. Talk with your family or friends about how you can work together to benefit the environment. Donate to an environmental preservation non-profit organization. Start an environmental stewardship group at your church.

HOLOCAUST REMEMBRANCE DAY

OUT of all of America's most solemn holidays, Holocaust Remembrance Day is perhaps the most sobering. It is not a day when we can celebrate; indeed, it is a day that commemorates one of the most horrifying events in human history: the systematic, genocidal slaughter of nearly six million Jews by Adolf Hitler and the Nazis during and before World War II from 1933 to 1945. Six million of God's chosen people. This incomprehensible number, representing more than a third of the Jews alive at the time, does not take into account the ruined lives of survivors who were left devastated after the carnage was finished. Nor does it include five million others who were killed in Europe during the period as Hitler pursued his despicable agenda of ridding Europe of all whom he considered undesirable, including the Roma people, then called Gypsies, and also Roman Catholics. The genocide against the Jews, however, was most successful and carried out primarily in six death camps in Poland.

For that reason, in 2005 the United Nations General Assembly proclaimed International Holocaust Remembrance Day to be January

27 because it is the anniversary of the liberation of Auschwitz-Birkenau, the largest Nazi death camp. In establishing International Holocaust Remembrance Day, the UN General Assembly was doing more than simply honoring the victims of the Nazi genocide and marking an horrific period in human history. It was also attempting to make certain that such genocide never occurs again. In that effort, the UN resolution creating IHRD obliges every nation in the UN to find ways to honor the victims; provide educational programs designed to prevent genocide; reject any denial of the Holocaust; and condemn discrimination and violence based on religion or ethnicity.

The date of the American Holocaust Remembrance Day varies depending upon the Hebrew calendar. Usually in April or May, the American Days of Remembrance are set to correspond with the Hebrew calendar's 27th day of Nisan which marks the anniversary of the Warsaw Ghetto uprising of 1943.

In enacting the Days of Remembrance as our nation's annual observance, the United States Congress also established the Holocaust Memorial Museum as a way—and a place—to permanently memorialize the victims and give families, friends, and all Americans a solemn, sacred space. Congress has also charged the

Museum with leading the nation in ceremonies and observances on the Days of Remembrance and throughout the year.

There are many obvious reasons why the Days of Remembrance are so deeply felt by Americans. Unlike many events in our history, there are a number of living Americans who remember the nightmare of the Holocaust. There are Jewish American families who lost loved ones in the genocide. Most of us have seen movies and read books about this 20th Century horror. Some of us have friends, neighbors, colleagues, and relatives who lived through this period, and we have heard their stories firsthand if we've been willing to listen.

But perhaps the most profound reason we remember the Holocaust is the one that is rarely articulated and most dreaded. The Holocaust provides the irrefutable evidence that evil can be born, live, grow, and flourish among us; it can even overwhelm us. The Holocaust is an agonizing reminder that, as Christians and Americans, we can never close our eyes to the presence of evil. We cannot tolerate it simply because it doesn't seem to impact us. It does impact us. If we allow it to exist, if we tolerate it, if we do not speak and act out against it, we turn away from the work Jesus gave us. And we become complicit.

PRAYER

GOD of Abraham, Isaac, and Jacob; Father of Jesus; Lord from Whom the Holy Spirit flows, strengthen us! Give us the foresight and the insight to recognize evil in all its insidious forms. Open our eyes when we wish to close them. Open our ears when we try not to listen. Open our minds when we struggle to keep them closed. Grant us the courage to speak and act against evil even when we appear to be at a safe distance from it. Help us to remember that when any one of Your children suffers because others look away, we all fail in our Christian duty. Amen.

ACTIVITY

FIND an event in your area that commemorates the Holocaust. Check the internet, local papers, synagogue web sites. Attend the event, if possible with a relative, friend, or colleague. If you cannot attend such an event, rent a movie such as *Schindler's List* or *Sophie's Choice*, read a book about the Holocaust, or read the posts at an on-line site about the Holocaust. Consider a time in your life when you have not stood up against evil in some form and pray to St. Maximilian Kolbe that you will do it differently next time.

MAY 1

SAINT JOSEPH THE WORKER

IN America, the ideals of Fatherhood and Labor are about as important and revered as Motherhood and apple pie. There is perhaps no nation on earth, except possibly for China, where hard work is valued more than it is in the United States. In our nation, labor is valued not only in and of itself, but for the dignity inherent in work. We are the nation of Horatio Alger, where hard work is believed to be the antidote to everything from poverty to a disadvantaged background or ancestry. And not only is labor considered to be an antidote to our society's ills, it is the dignified price one pays for success. Even after the past few years of economic stress, there are few Americans who would declare that success at any level is possible without hard work.

Likewise, we Americans honor fatherhood and everything that is inherent in that ideal: strength, commitment, protection of innocence, guidance, family stability, provision, leadership, and patience. We expect fathers to provide all of these, and more; and right or wrong, we tend to believe that children without fathers—or strong father-figures—are at a disadvantage in the wide world. Almost all of our presidents have been fathers, and much is made of the families of American leaders, as if the strength of a man's family is a measure of the man.

You could say that in this country, fatherhood and hard work go hand-in-hand. Whether and how a man provides for his family is perceived as another measure of the man, even in these times, when the provider in a family is just as likely to be a mother. In the family unit, what we value most highly is a partnership between the husband and wife; and in this, as in all these characteristics, Joseph, the human foster father of Jesus and the husband of Mary, is the embodiment of perfection. Selected by God to protect and nurture His only-begotten Son and the woman chosen to bear Him, Joseph represents all that is good and pure in fatherhood and labor.

Willing to risk his reputation in his community and his reputation as a man; willing to submit to the ridicule of appearing to be soft-hearted and committed to a much younger woman who seemed to have betrayed him; willing to follow dreams and visions that would take him away from everything that was familiar and beloved by him; willing to ply the hard trade of carpentry in towns and nations unknown to him, Joseph was ever self-sacrificing. Knowing what we know now, it is easy to elevate him to a status beyond anything the people of his time would have imagined. Indeed, in his day, he was likely seen as something of a fool, laboring hard every day of his life for a woman who married him while pregnant with Another's Child, and for that very Child who would eventually turn from his earthly father's life to answer an entirely different call.

And yet, today, we know who Joseph was. We know that there is no better model of selfless fatherhood and dignified labor. We know that if fathers today followed the example of Joseph, instead of their own ambitions and egos, America would be a much stronger country. We know that if workers toiled with the commitment and strength of Joseph, the dignity inherent in daily work would resume its rightful place in America.

People of faith in the United States rightly celebrate Joseph for both of his essential roles: as father and worker. Although March 19 is the Feast of St. Joseph in the Catholic Church where he is Patron of the Universal Church, he is also honored on May 1 for his role as St. Joseph the Worker. May 1 was chosen as a Christian statement of the godliness of work to counter the original communist festival of

labor on that day. Revering Joseph as a dignified worker is also a way for people of faith
to note that work doesn't have to produce
wealth —for Joseph was never a rich man—to
be of great value. Quite the contrary, as Joseph
proves: the value of a decent working life is not
measured by how much that life earns. Joseph
is also considered Patron of the Mystical Body
of Christ because of the wonderful way he
fulfilled his duty as Jesus' foster-father; Patron
of Christian Schools for his role in raising
Jesus; and Patron of a Happy Death because
he died surrounded by Jesus and Mary, and it
is believed that all who seek Joseph at the hour
of their own deaths will be comforted.

PRAYER

JOSEPH, unlike Jesus and Mary, you were
just like us. You were not God's only begot-
ten Son, and yet you were created to raise and
protect and guide in human ways, God's Son.
You were not born without sin, and yet you
were created to be husband to a woman born
without sin. In theory, then, you were just like
us, and yet, how often can we say we are just
like you? Help us, foster father of Jesus and
husband of Mary, to be loving spouses, good
parents, and diligent workers. Guide us to do
the labor God gives us, in our families and in

our workplaces, without complaints or self-pity. Strengthen us with the patience to accept our lot in life and follow the path God has set us on. Amen.

ACTIVITY

TODAY, try to emulate St. Joseph. If you are a parent, make an extra effort to be patient and gentle. Pray for the strength to be the kind of parent you know you should be and not necessarily the kind of parent that the stress and pressure of life may push you into being. Remind yourself that there is a divine spark in every child and do your best to respond to the love of Christ that is in your child (even if it is well-hidden!). Whatever your work may be, approach it today from the perspective of Joseph: with uncomplaining industriousness and your best effort. Be conscious during the day of how difficult it can be to achieve these simple ideals and thank God for the model of St. Joseph. Say this short prayer in his honor.

DEAR St. Joseph, you are an outstanding model of one who strove for holiness every day of your life on earth. Obtain for us the grace to strive for Christian perfection in all that we do or say. Help us to keep the commandments of God and of his holy church and to practice the evangelical counsels in the way that applies to our state in life.

Give us such an awareness of God's mercies that with truly thankful hearts we may show forth his praise, not only with our lips, but also in our lives. Let us give ourselves to his service and walk before him in holiness and righteousness all our days.

May we then attain to that holiness which you and Mary now enjoy with all the Saints in the presence of the Blessed Trinity.

MAY, SECOND SUNDAY
MOTHER'S DAY

IT probably shouldn't be too astonishing that the origins of Mother's Day are more about the service by mothers than the serving *of* them. In 1870, Julia Ward Howe wrote the "Mother's Day Proclamation," and it was a far cry from a demand that mothers be honored and coddled one day a year. On the contrary, Ward Howe's statement was an affirmation of all that mothers do and give; it was written as a reaction to the devastation of the American Civil War and the Franco-Prussian war, and it attested to the agonizing sacrifices mothers and wives make, especially during wartime. Ward Howe believed that women had an important role to play politically in American society, and that mothers would be the natural leaders in assuming that role.

Ann Jarvis agreed with her. She followed up on Ward Howe's Mother's Day Proclamation by taking action. If anything, Jarvis moved even further away from the concept of Mother's Day as a day of leisure by establishing five Mothers' Day Work Clubs. Women who joined these disciplined clubs were charged with the difficult work of improving sanitary and health conditions in their communities. Ann

Jarvis died in 1905, but her daughter, Anna, took up the cause. In 1907, Anna Jarvis held a memorial gathering for her mother and began working to make "Mother's Day" a recognized holiday in the United States. By 1914, she'd succeeded, but in typical fashion Anna followed in her mother and Ward Howe's footsteps; she'd wanted the day to reflect and honor the work done by mothers. When it didn't, in the 1920s she declared herself disappointed with the commercialism that already attended the holiday.

Granted, we think of Mother's Day today as a day to honor and even pamper all Moms, but the fact that the day was inspired by the extraordinary service mothers provide to our families and nation is fitting. It also makes sense that Mother's Day is celebrated in various ways and on different dates all over the world. As Ward Howe pointed out, mothers are the ones forced to watch fathers, sons, husbands, and brothers go off to war; and mothers are the ones who must mourn silently and alone while trying to minimize the damage of war. Mothers are most called upon to do the hard work of building society, even as they were for the greater part of America's history, limited and marginalized because of gender. Perhaps because mothers have often been forced to watch from the political and economic sidelines, their role in shaping the future of this country has had to be even more committed and continuous. And now the role of women has become even more complex and dangerous as women—who are themselves mothers—enlist and go off to war or serve our country at home and abroad in all branches of military service.

In other words, for all that we appropriately celebrate them today, mothers suffer, and often silently. No mother illustrates this more than Mary, Jesus' mother. From giving birth in a cold cave; to the sting of hearing her Son respond to her request to see Him, by asking, "Who is my mother?" in front of a large crowd; to the piercing agony of watching Him crucified, Mary suffered. We have no evidence of even the mildest complaint. And yet she bore and raised the One who changed the world.

Every mother carries the burden of knowing that her actions, example, teaching, discipline, faith will have a great impact on family, community, and country. It is that burden that we honor more than anything today, and the willingness of mothers to assume this ponderous weight. Most women can bear a child, but it takes a mother, dedicated to her task, to raise children prepared to take on the mantle of a nation with resources and riches as numerous as its challenges.

PRAYER

FATHER of all mothers, today and always we ask You to bless and protect them. We praise You for giving us women strong enough to be good mothers, to contribute to the welfare of all children and our nation. We ask You to give them the strength for the hard and often thankless tasks, small and large, they take on every day. Forgive us when we hurt our mothers, consciously or unconsciously. For those of us who are responsible for children, teach us to be good and nurturing mothers. Forgive us when we fail and keep us close to You in all that we undertake with our children. Give us patience, strength, and peace as we carry our precious burden. Amen.

ACTIVITY

TODAY, do something for a mother who isn't yours. Of course, make sure you do something wonderful for your own mother: cards, gifts, flowers, dinner, all of the above. But in addition, consider the other women in your life who are mothers: neighbors, sisters, cousins, colleagues, bank tellers, deli workers, grocery store cashiers. Once you start to think about it, the list will probably be long. Select one (or more) of these women, and recognize them in some way. Give a present. Offer to baby-sit or to cook dinner and set a night that is convenient for her. Make an effort to do this even if you are a mother yourself.

MAY, THIRD SATURDAY
ARMED FORCES DAY

WHILE the United States of America has several festivals and federal holidays honoring veterans and the war dead, or marking particular anniversaries and victories in military history, Armed Forces Day is the one day when we recognize the individuals *and* institutions that work to protect our nation. Celebrated every year on the third Saturday of May, Armed Forces Day also caps off Armed Forces Week which begins on the second Saturday of every May and ends on the third Sunday of the month.

Until 1949 each branch of the U.S. Military Service had its own day of recognition. However, with the unifying of all "Armed Services" under the U.S. Department of Defense, there was a push to establish one holiday. Although the Army, Navy, Coast Guard and Air Force agreed to adopt a single day, the Marine Corps opted to continue their separate celebration while also supporting the new, unified Armed Forces Day. Within each branch of service, the original days are still remembered.

The first Armed Services Day was officially celebrated the following year in 1950 with the intention of showing the American public that the various services were truly committed to unification. With a central theme called "Teamed for Defense," the festival—and the preceding week—was designed to help Americans become comfortable with the idea of all branches of service under one central power, the Department of Defense. Coming not long after World War II, the week also focused on showing Americans what role a unified military could play during peace time and in civilian life.

That initial Armed Forces Day in 1950 was, in many ways, a time for all Americans to breathe a collective sigh of relief. World War II was over, the members of the Armed Forces were mostly home or protecting the peace in Europe, and the theme of unification was echoed in many aspects of American life from families that had come together again after the war, to businesses that were collaborating and growing with a vastly improved economy. The original Armed Forces Day celebrations included open houses at military and government facilities, parades, receptions, and air shows. It was and continues to be a day when the military gets to demonstrate its readiness— through personnel and high-tech equipment— to protect the nation.

Over the years posters and other artwork created to promote various Armed Forces

Days have depicted service men and women in uniform and with their families, often with backdrops that include the American flag and other patriotic images. These posters have become collectors' items for many and have reflected annual Armed Services Day themes such as Appreciation of a Nation, Dedication and Devotion, Freedom Through Unity, Liberty, Power for Peace, and Prepared to Meet the Challenge.

Clearly, the overriding purpose of Armed Services Day—in 1950 and today—is to allow service members to demonstrate their pride in and dedication to their work and to assure Americans that the various branches of the military are working as a unified force to protect and defend the nation. Coming on the heels of World War II, this sense of comfort and unity was profoundly important to the American people and was a sign to the rest of the world that America stood with its troops.

In 1962, in the face of another grave threat, this time from Russia during the Cold War, President John F. Kennedy proclaimed Armed Forces Day as an official holiday.

PRAYER

GOD Who is our only true defense, please protect the men and women and institutions that serve our country. Keep them safe from harm in their work and in their daily lives. Give them work that builds up rather than tears down. Guard their souls and their minds from stress and anger. Guide them on a path of honor, decency, and compassion in all that they do. Give them the courage to act with integrity. Forgive them when they feel compelled by duty's call to break Your laws. Ease their minds and hearts and give them rest in You. Protect and bless their families. Help our political and military leaders to avoid war and destruction, and to seek opportunities for peace and cooperation. Amen.

ACTIVITY

THERE are many, many organizations that have been created with the objective of supporting American service men and women. If you do not already contribute to such an organization, find one that you are comfortable with and send money or volunteer. A number of them will also give you the opportunity to write to an individual who is currently serving or has served in the Armed Forces. Write a note expressing your appreciation for his or her contribution and your commitment to keep her or him in your prayers.

MAY, LAST MONDAY
MEMORIAL DAY

FOR a national holiday that has, at its heart, the objective of overcoming our differences in order to honor all Americans who have died in wars, Memorial Day had somewhat contentious beginnings. Nearly 30 towns and cities compete for the right to claim that they were the first to establish what was originally called Decoration Day. Also somewhat ironically for a day that signifies American unity in recognizing the war dead, it is most likely that Memorial Day got its start during—or as a result of—the Civil War, which was the most painful and divisive war in our history. In Duke University's Historic American Sheet Music, 1850-1920, there is a song called "Kneel Where Our Loved Ones are Sleeping," by Nella L. Sweet, dedicated to "The Ladies of the South who are Decorating the Graves of the Confederate Dead."

Memorial Day was first officially proclaimed in 1868, shortly after the Civil War. In an attempt to finally settle the matter of where the holiday actually originated, President Lyndon B. Johnson in 1966 declared Waterloo, New York, as its official birthplace. The reality is that for many years, individuals and groups from all over the country have had formal and informal ways and rituals for showing respect to friends and relatives who had died during American wars.

Regardless of where or precisely how Memorial Day got its start, it has come to be a day in which Americans recognize those who have given their lives in service to the country, traditionally by cleaning up and/or decorating their graves. Communities and municipalities often have ceremonies at graveyards or war monuments, usually erected in the town green or square. Parades, laying of wreaths and flowers on graves or symbolic sites, church and religious services, and the reading of the names of the dead are all traditions that mark the day.

Memorial Day is a wonderful example of America at its best . . . and its most honest. While Americans have disagreed on the causes and objectives of wars from the War for Independence, where a number of colonists wanted to remain under England, to the War on Terror, we all agree that the men and women who have died serving America should, and must, be honored. It is a day for reflection, a day to consider what we want and need as a country, and to weigh the great cost of achieving our objectives. It is a day to remind ourselves that in every war "victory," there is also tremendous loss. In the end, Memorial Day should be a day of healing, a day when we put aside our political and philosophical differences to acknowledge that we are one nation, and that every time we lose a person to war, we have lost part of ourselves, and therefore, need to grieve, heal, honor, and go on. Together.

PRAYER

JESUS, lover of peace, You preached love and conciliation, all the time knowing that our human natures lean toward division and war. Even as You urged us to love, heal and forgive each other, You knew there would be times when we would do the opposite. You knew that our needs and our fears and our anger would lead us in a direction that could threaten to pull us away from You. Forgive us, Lord, for the times that our fears overwhelm our faith. Thank You for the gift of this day, a day when we can join together and remember those we've lost. Remind us, in the midst of today's pageantry and parades, of the families who still mourn and struggle to recover. Increase our faith and remind us to live our lives according to the Gospels. Draw us closer to You, Jesus, and take those who have sacrificed everything for America into Your loving embrace. Amen.

ACTIVITY

CELEBRATE Memorial Day twice: once with others and once privately. For your community celebration, go to a church service, a town or city memorial program, a parade, a wreath-laying ceremony, or a similar public presentation. For your private time, write a "letter" to a person who has died in the service of America. If you have a friend, relative or ancestor who has died in a war or war action, write a letter saying everything you would like to say to that person but didn't have the chance to communicate. Tell the person about yourself now, what you think and how you feel about war. Describe how that person's death has impacted you and your outlook. If no one related or close to you has died in America's service, find the name of—and, if possible, a little information on—someone who has died. Write that individual a letter thanking him or her for making the ultimate sacrifice. Describe how you want to live your life in recognition of, and as a result of, that sacrifice. Keep the letter as your own memorial.

WALT WHITMAN'S BIRTHDAY

WALTER Whitman, born on May 31, 1819, was the perfect American in that . . . there is no such thing! Whitman was a little bit of everything, resembling in his person and life the patchwork quilt that is America. Unlike other 19th century American literary figures, many of whom tended to be a relatively genteel and moneyed lot, Whitman was born into relative poverty and yet managed to rise so high in the estimation of his eventual peers that men like Henry David Thoreau and Ralph Waldo Emerson sought him out. How to accurately describe Walt Whitman? That is really a multiple choice question. Controversial poet who later was referred to as the father of free verse. Journalist. Teacher. Government clerk. Egalitarian. Humanist. Transcendentalist. Civil War Army Nurse. Promoter of Temperance. Printer. Publisher. Editor. The answer to the question of "Who was Walt Whitman?" is, of course, all of the above . . . and then some.

To put it bluntly, Whitman was like America in that he was all over the place! A restless soul who lived most of his life straining against the bonds of poverty, Whitman was constantly searching for truth and beauty. However, he was hardly a writer with his head in the clouds. While striving to be an aesthetic on one hand, Whitman was deeply concerned with political matters and the grittier aspects of life. He made references all his life and throughout his written work of his impoverished origins. And whatever profession he happened to be pursuing at any given time, he was painfully aware of the need to make a living.

Though he worked off and on during his whole life as a journalist and writer, Whitman is best known for his poetry. A volunteer nurse during the Civil War, Whitman was deeply moved by the suffering he witnessed and wrote movingly of it. Prior to witnessing the ravages of the war, Whitman's poem, "Beat! Beat! Drums," had been a rallying call for the abolitionist north. But the works he produced as a result of his time in the hospital wards were more sober and included, "The Great Army of the Sick," and "Memoranda During the War." His poem, "O Captain! My Captain," a tribute to Abraham Lincoln upon his death, won Whitman even greater renown.

Leaves of Grass is the lifelong work which he published in many editions and was constantly fine-tuning at various points in his life. In this work Whitman set out to produce an American epic poem, using a rhythm based on Biblical verse. America had never seen anything like the great poetic work that he did, indeed, produce, and some readers were offended by Whitman's refusal to be limited by the morality of the time. But in many ways *Leaves of Grass* did truly describe the diversity of America, perhaps best reflected in Whitman's description of himself in the poem: "Walt Whitman, one of the roughs, a kosmos, disorderly, fleshly, and sensual, no sentimentalist, no stander above men or women or apart from them, no more modest than immodest." The poem, like the country, was bold and forthright, winning Whitman both praise and condemnation.

It was Whitman's dearest hope to reach the common American with *Leaves of Grass* and, if his popularity was any measure, that he certainly did: after he died from a variety of ailments in 1892, the public was allowed to view his body at his Camden, New Jersey, home, and over a thousand people rushed to the house in the first three hours. The casket was so utterly covered with flowers and wreaths, that it was difficult to even see the body. A few days later, Whitman was celebrated and honored by some of the leading men and women of the arts, government, and literature. He had, by the end of his life, created a community of friends and readers that knew no boundaries.

PRAYER

JESUS, You commanded us to love one another as we love ourselves. We thank You for the example of people like Walt Whitman, who, despite facing many difficulties in his life, managed to obey that commandment. Remind us that we cannot give up just because it isn't easy or convenient to love. Teach us that love is an action, and not just a concept. Help us to reach across the boundaries of race, gender, and social status to touch the hearts of all Your people. Let us persevere in communicating Your love especially during times of strife and sorrow. Amen.

ACTIVITY

LIKE Walt Whitman, America is a grand tapestry of influences, politics, religions, races, and philosophies. Whitman tried to express the greatness and diversity of 19th Century America in his poetry. Write a poem (it doesn't have to rhyme!) that expresses the greatness and diversity of 21st Century America. Be bold and honest like Whitman. And like Whitman, be compassionate and empathetic as well. In finishing the poem, describe your vision of America at its best.

JUNE 14

FLAG DAY

FLAG Day is a uniquely American holiday. While all nations, not to mention
states, universities and other institutions, have
their own flags, America's celebration of The
Stars and Stripes is a profoundly felt national
expression of the pride and hope we invest in
the United States of America. The American
flag, with its red stripes representing the blood
spilled in defense of the country; the blue representing the aspirations of an endless, open
sky; and the white stars, one for every state,
is a revered symbol for most Americans of
all that our nation has in the past, does now,
and will in the future represent. The fact that
Flag Day's history goes all the way back to the
earliest days of Independence, even before the
war against Britain was won, is evidence of the
banner's importance.

What we remember today is that on June 14,
1777, the Second Continental Congress issued a
resolution adopting the flag of the United States
of America . . . even before there was an official
United States. Flag Day is also the birthday of
the United States Army, an event that predated
even the adoption of the flag. On June 14, 1775,
the Committee of the Whole in Congress adopted "the American continental army," creating

the military institution that would defend the flag and that still exists today. During World War I President Woodrow Wilson issued a proclamation officially establishing June 14 as Flag Day, and in 1949, after World War II, an Act of Congress named the date as National Flag Day although it has never been made an official federal holiday.

From all of this, it would be logical to assume that the United States flag is perceived mostly as a symbol of America at war, but this is not the case. While the flag is certainly a prominent visual emblem during all the processes of war—from the politicians making the decisions in Washington, to the soldiers on the march—"Old Glory" is also an important presence in schools, municipal buildings, places of worship, and many homes. And while the flag may serve slightly different purposes in each of these—and many other—institutions, it may always be seen as a declaration of what unites us as a people, rather than what divides us. We need only glimpse the American flag at half-mast to feel a stab of sorrow, sometimes even before we know who or what has caused it to be flown at half-mast. Flags drape the coffins of those who have served in the American military, even if they lived a long life afterward. The Stars and Stripes flutter at sporting events, and perhaps most importantly at the Olympics, one of the last remaining events that seek to bring nations together.

Though Flag Day is not a federal holiday, it is a sign of how strongly we feel about our nation's flag that some of the oldest, largest, and longest parades in the American calendar occur on this holiday. Quincy, Massachusetts, once in the heart of Revolutionary War territory, has been hosting a Flag Day parade for over 60 years; and the largest Flag Day parade is held every year in Troy, New York, often drawing as many as 50,000 spectators. Fairfield, Washington, has held an annual Flag Day parade for over 100 years.

Why is this relatively simple piece of cloth so important to us? For many Americans it represents not just the best of our country, but also the fact that we are "one nation under God," as we say in our Pledge of Allegiance to the Flag. Our flag is a symbol of inclusion, an image that changed (its design and its number of stars) as we grew as a nation. It did not remain rigid and unbending, even as it continued to proclaim America as a great experiment based on Judeo-Christian ideals.

PRAYER

GOD over all nations and flags, we thank You for providing us with this symbol of our independence from human power, our refusal to be ruled by any man. We praise You for this banner which flies in a nation and under the skies that You created. We thank You for the changes in it over the years, changes that demonstrate our generosity and openness of spirit. We ask You to keep the people who raise this symbol safe and prosperous, so that we will be better able to do Your work with the resources You have provided us. Unite us, Father, under Your care and guidance. Help us to become a nation that lives up to the promise of our flag in everything we do. Teach us to—in this order—honor You, honor each other, and honor our country. Amen.

PRAYER FOR OUR COUNTRY

HEAVENLY Father, You are the real foundation of nations, raising them up to serve and care for the people dwelling in their boundaries. I thank You for making me a citizen of this land of freedom and unlimited opportunity—which are the result of its Christian base. Send forth Your Spirit to this country and make it a source of wisdom and strength, order and integrity throughout the world.

ACTIVITY

IF you were to create a flag for the United States, what would it look like? Would you use the same colors? How would you design it? What would you try to represent on that piece of cloth? What shape would you make it? What would you want people to feel and think when they saw it? Consider all these questions, and then get paper and colored pencils (or paint or markers) and design your own American flag. Look at it periodically throughout the year and think about whether and how you would change it as events in America unfold.

JUNE, THIRD SUNDAY
FATHER'S DAY

LET'S face it: this is one holiday that suffers from gender bias. When it comes to parental holidays, it's all about Mom. Dad usually gets short shrift. The elaborate cards, flowers, candies, breakfasts-in-bed, cappuccino makers, and other gorgeously wrapped presents of last month are long gone, replaced—*maybe*— by a tasteful (or not so tasteful) tie, nose hair trimmers, hedge clippers, and an Egg McMuffin. That's if Dad's lucky. Not so lucky fathers? They are feted with—maybe—athletic socks, goofy cards (probably not even Hallmark), tie clips, jokey suspenders, or a bowl of bran flakes and skim milk. The truly unlucky fathers get zip.

Just how low on the parental holiday status does Father's Day rate? Well, it was not even a glimmer in anyone's eye when Mother's Day was officially established. The first unofficial Father's Day was anything but a national event, observed on June 19, 1910, by a diligent daughter (who, by the way, had a mother long deceased, which is not to suggest she was tired of missing out on Mother's Day). Mrs. John B. Dodd wanted to honor her father, a Civil War veteran and single parent who raised his six children, including Mrs. Dodd, after his wife died in childbirth. He selflessly and quietly took on this monumental task while also running his family's farm in Washington state.

From then, Father's Day caught on. Sort of. A few other towns and cities around America began picking up on the idea, and in 1924 President Calvin Coolidge endorsed the idea of a national Father's Day. There is no mention of the greeting card lobby in the history of this endorsement and, in fact, it must have been a pretty tepid endorsement because Father's Day did not become an official American holiday until 1966 when President Lyndon Johnson signed a proclamation fixing the date on the third Sunday of June. Probably Ladybird made him do it.

The great thing about fathers is that they really don't seem to mind this lack of adulation, or even attention. They're OK with Mom getting the limelight. Most of them just plow ahead like Mrs. Dodd's father, that good, reliable farmer, veteran, and single father who got the whole thing started. Fathers, the best of them, work hard, support their families, worry about money and college and boyfriends, play with their kids when the kids allow it, and love their wives. And despite their country being somewhat slow to recognize them, fathers, and their wives, form the backbone of America.

They don't crow about it. They don't ask for much. They just get the job done.

Remind you of Anyone?

Yes, the great fathers take God as their model. And what a model! Loving, forgiving, healing, ever-patient, strong, understanding, constantly working, God is the ultimate Father. While no human father can come close to our divine Father, the best fathers are those who hold the example of God in their hearts and seek always to emulate Him.

Just as many of us take our fathers for granted, we sometimes do the same with God. And God, like many of our human dads, asks very little of us. Still, we should guard against such lack of consideration. Today reminds us to give our Heavenly Father thanks for everything He's given us, including our earthly fathers.

PRAYER

GOD and Father, it is true that no earthly parent can measure up to You. Thank You for those fathers who try. Thank You for the dads who work hard to follow Your example and do Your work. We praise You for giving them to us and our nation. We ask You to protect, nurture and encourage them, especially when we are slow to do so. Remind us to show our appreciation. Teach us how to lighten their burdens and ease their way. Help us to support them. Show us how to forgive those fathers who are unable to be the men we need them to be. Give us the gift of compassion and understanding. And let us never stop praising and glorifying You, our most perfect heavenly Father. Amen.

ACTIVITY

SPEND some time with both your Dads today. Set aside a special time for prayer, communicating openly with God, your heavenly Father. Tell Him about your life, hopes, dreams, work, worries. Sure, He already knows, but, like many Fathers, He might like to hear it directly from you. Ask Him for help where you need it, and thank Him for stability where you don't. Then, turn to your earthly dad. If he is living, call or visit. If you haven't already sent a card, send one even if it's late. He's probably used to it. Better yet, send him flowers or fruit or candy or those thick Omaha steaks. He's probably *not* used to that! If your father has died, visit his grave or another quiet place and hold him in your heart. To yourself or aloud, say the things you'd like to say to him if he were with you. If you need to forgive him, do it now. If you need forgiveness from him, ask for it from him and from God. Be at peace knowing that at least one of your Fathers, and probably both, forgives you.

FIRST DAY OF SUMMER

TODAY—or yesterday, depending on the year and the precise planetary readings—is the longest day of the year, the first day of summer, otherwise known as the Summer Solstice. For the United States and other countries in the Northern Hemisphere, this means that the sun is positioned as far north in relation to the earth as it will be all year. Although it may seem that we are closer to the sun today, the fact is that the earth is closest to the sun in December during the Winter Solstice. Both Summer and Winter Solstices occur as a result of how the earth is tilted in relation to the sun.

For me, the first day of summer has always been a day to decide between whether the glass is half full or half empty. On the one hand, what could be better than the first day of summer? When I was young, I yearned for the end of the school year with a passion, and by June 21, it was usually over. The first day of summer represents everything good: freedom, long days of sunlight, time (even for adults!) to play, read, go to the beach. On the other hand, the first day of summer is the longest day of the year, and since I tend to be at least as pessimistic as I am optimistic, that means that it's all downhill from here. If I really want to concentrate on the downside, I can even track the loss of light every evening, minute-by-minute, on the weather page in my local newspaper. Sure, we have three solid months of summer in front of us, but every passing day means a tiny loss that will soon add up.

My guess is that this is not how God wants us to look at the gift of this day, the gift of summer. Americans seem mostly to get it right: today is a day to rejoice over. Today starts the season of fun and freedom, sunlight and parades, picnics and barbecues, biking and boating, hammocks and beach chairs, baseball and badminton, tennis and golf. Americans will celebrate the next 90 days with outdoor concerts on town greens, trips to the beach and pool, backyard stargazing, July 4th fireworks, church fairs, long walks, visits to national monuments and parks, Shakespeare in the park, and family vacations. We will admire the single-mindedness of robins, take note of the industry of ant colonies and bee hives, and shoo seagulls away from our french fries. We will go out for fried clams and hot dogs and ice cream. We will run through sprinklers, wash our cars, and eat strawberries. Summer is a time to come together, to bask in the warmth of the sun and the companionship of those we love and our neighbors. It is a time to reach out, to take a risk, to show kindness, to open our hearts. It is a time to move our bodies, to appreciate nature, to celebrate all the colors and flavors and abundance of America.

Summer is a time to count our blessings. The glass is, indeed, more than half full. It is overflowing with God's gifts.

PRAYER

FATHER, we thank You for the glorious gift—and manifold gifts—of summer. We thank You for this long, languorous day and the opportunity to choose to enjoy every minute of it. We ask You for the grace to make good use of this season stretching ahead of us. We ask You for the energy and time and enthusiasm to enjoy every moment. We ask You to bless our plans . . . or give us better ones! We ask You to bring us together as friends, family members, colleagues, teams, parishes, communities; and most importantly, as a nation blessed abundantly by You. Amen.

ACTIVITY

GET out your calendar and make a plan to do something "summery" for every week of the season. Don't set impossible goals and don't make it a competition to see if you can outdo yourself every week. Keep your plans simple. Read a novel one week. Go to a parade another week. Shop at a local farmers' market the next. Watch a fireworks display. Get a schedule and take a ferry ride. Lie in a hammock. Go to the beach. Search for a constellation in the night sky. Stroll along a beach or trail. Ask someone to join you in all or any of these ventures. Ask God to bless your plans and give you a fulfilling summer.

JULY 1

HARRIET BEECHER STOWE
ANNIVERSARY

HARRIET Beecher Stowe embodied the intersection of church and state in America. At no point in her long, spirited, courageous life did the words "separation of church and state" apply to her; and yet, she was and remains one of the staunchest, strongest and most patriotic figures in American literature and history.

The seventh of 13 children, Harriet Beecher was born in Litchfield, Connecticut, on June 14, 1811, into an extremely religious family. Many of her brothers became ministers. Though a renowned and established religious leader, Lyman Beecher, Beecher Stowe's father, was progressive in many ways; his daughters were educated in traditionally male disciplines, studying the classics, languages, and mathematics. Because of her family's social and religious position, Beecher Stowe was exposed to the best and most forward-thinking minds in the country from a young age. After following her father to Cincinnati, Ohio, where he'd assumed the presidency of Lane Theological School, Beecher Stowe joined a literary and social community where she met her husband, Calvin Ellis Stowe. He was a widower and professor at her father's seminary and a fervent abolitionist.

She was drawn to his fierce opposition to slavery, and after they married in 1836, she joined him in supporting the Underground Railroad for runaway slaves, and they occasionally housed fugitive slaves in their home. The Stowes had seven children, though Harriet continued to pursue her writing and an unwavering anti-slavery agenda. In 1850 when Congress passed the Fugitive Slave Law, which made it illegal to help runaway slaves, Beecher Stowe sharpened her pen. She arranged with Gamaliel Baily, the editor of a weekly anti-slavery journal called "National Era," to write a story in installments that would reveal the inhumanity of slavery. In explaining her decision to pursue this controversial course of action, Beecher Stowe wrote, "even a woman or a child who can speak a word for freedom and humanity is bound to speak . . . I hope every woman who can write will not be silent."

From June 5, 1851 to April 1, 1852, the infamous book that came to be called *Uncle Tom's Cabin* was published weekly in "National Era." Fittingly for a book that revealed the desperation of slavery, Beecher Stowe originally gave her book the subtitle, "The Man That Was A Thing." When it was published in March, 1852 in book form, *Uncle Tom's Cabin* became an instant American classic, selling over 300,000 copies in a year.

Eventually, the novel and play were read and/or seen by millions, and Beecher Stowe's reputation grew exponentially. Not all readers were pleased. She was despised in the American South for her heartrending depiction of slavery which turned many Americans who had been on the fence over slavery against it. In the north and in the United Kingdom, she was praised and considered by many to be the single-most important, white anti-slavery voice in the nation. On November 25, 1862, during the Civil War, Harriet Beecher Stowe was invited to the White House, and one description of her meeting with the President says that Abraham Lincoln greeted her with, "So you are the little woman who wrote the book that started this great war."

Whether this is true or not, there is no question that Harriet Beecher Stowe had a tremendous influence on how America and the world perceived the despicable institution of slavery. She published over 20 books and was a vocal supporter of human rights and other sometimes unpopular issues during the 85 years of her life. For Christians, she remains a stunning model of righteousness, living her faith so publicly and politically that she could not be ignored.

PRAYER

GOD Who is Spirit, Truth and Life, fill us with the courage we need to break free from our failings and limitations and speak Your truth. Make us righteous, Lord! Bring people into our lives who will support and encourage us and give us opportunities to do Your work. Help us to lead by our words and our actions. Let us not hold back our hands or silence our tongues when, by reaching out or speaking, we can help another. Give us the strength to not simply speak of Christianity but to live Christianity. Amen.

ACTIVITY

DO you judge by appearances or just a few of the facts? It is easy to do. Take Harriet Beecher Stowe. The facts of her life were that she was born to a nationally known religious preacher and teacher, one of many children; her mother died when she was five; her brothers became ministers; she dutifully followed her father wherever his work took him, and then she dutifully followed her husband wherever his work took him, bearing him seven children in the process. What they believed, she believed. She lived during a time when women were all but powerless in government and religion. And yet, she virtually changed the world. Observe the people in your life today: colleagues, postal deliverer, your child's teacher, even your family members. Do you think you know all there is to know about them? Do you believe you know their achievements and limitations? Do you think they know all there is to know about you?

PASSAGE OF
THE CIVIL RIGHTS ACT

A CENTURY after the American Civil War ended, what Abraham Lincoln might well have accomplished had he lived, was finally achieved in America. When President Lyndon B. Johnson signed the Civil Rights Act of 1964 on July 2, he effectively made racial equality the law of the land. The Act provided the legal guarantee that all Americans, regardless of race, would be treated equally. Specifically, the law banned discrimination in many aspects of American life including businesses like theaters, hotels and restaurants; public places such as schools, swimming pools, beaches, and libraries; employment; and housing.

The concept and creation of a Civil Rights Act was first expressed by President John F. Kennedy over a year earlier in a nationally televised address where he urged the American people to put an end to inequality based on race wherever it still existed. And despite the best intentions of Lincoln and many who came after him, racism did still exist in many areas of American life. Indeed, it was not easy to get the Act passed despite Kennedy's plea and subsequent assassination. Extreme efforts were made in both houses of Congress to block the bill, and it was only through the herculean efforts of Senators Hubert Humphrey and Everett Dirksen, and President Johnson's strong support, that the Act was pushed through. Johnson signed it on the same day, just hours after it made it out of Congress, almost as if he thought they might still stop it!

Since its passage, the Civil Rights Act has been invoked in many situations, expanding beyond the original intent to end race-based discrimination. Today we frequently hear people who feel wronged because of their gender or lifestyle choices claim that their Civil Rights have been infringed upon. In fact, the complete definition of Civil Rights also encompasses the Thirteenth Amendment, which abolished slavery, and the Fourteenth Amendment, which prevents government from denying citizens life, liberty and property without due process of law and also provides for no taxation without representation.

What should the words Civil Rights mean to American Christians? The dictionary has almost half-a-page devoted to the definition, and while civil refers to civilization, or the citizenry of a nation, it is also a synonym for courteous, polite, chivalrous, and gallant. To be civil, to act with civility, is to treat others with decency and respect. So, the word that is frequently used to suggest how government should be conducted can also be used to describe how a Christian should conduct him- or herself. For people of faith living in the United States, Civil Rights for all is a concept rooted in the Judeo-Christian tradition and scripture. It is a Gospel imperative articulated by Jesus when He taught us to love one another as we love ourselves. In the practice of Civil Rights in America—church and state are not separated; they come together to truly form a more perfect union.

PRAYER

CREATOR of all that is civil and good, we praise You for giving us a nation with laws that mirror and support those that You provided. Help us to be civil, to be Christian, in our spirits as well as by the law. Teach us what it means to love one another, regardless of who the other is or what the other looks like. Jesus, You taught us that our neighbor whom we are to love can be found in every person we encounter. As we go through our lives, strengthen us to love. Inculcate in us the spiritual civility that finds its expression in courteous, polite, and kind behavior, all in Your precious name. Caution us, as You did the Pharisees and scribes, against adhering to the letter of the law while abrogating its spirit. Gird us to face the world with our hearts, minds, spirits, eyes, and ears all open and ready to love. Amen.

ACTIVITY

ARE you a civil Christian? Think back over the past year. Examine all aspects of your life—your work, your church, your family, your friends, your enemies. Have you been civil in Christian spirit as well as by American law? Ask yourself if you've discriminated against anyone because of how they look or act. Have you ever used what power you may have—as a supervisor, a customer, a parent, a spouse, a cleric, a teacher—to bully or denigrate someone? In other words, have you ever robbed someone of their civil rights? Were you aware of what you were doing when you were doing it? As you consider a time or times when you've been uncivil, unChristian, examine how you were feeling at the time. Were you angry, fearful, resentful? Did you act out of arrogance or ignorance? In America, it is illegal to take away a person's civil rights, and restitution must be made. Before God, it is also wrong. Ask God to forgive you and show you a way to make adequate restitution and to learn from your uncivil behavior to prevent it in the future.

JULY 4

INDEPENDENCE DAY

HISTORIANS, not to mention history teachers, bemoan the lack of knowledge many Americans demonstrate when it comes to their nation's history. But one day that even most of the youngest American children can usually name and describe is July 4th, the day America declared its independence from the British empire. No longer would America accept the rule of an English king. Indeed, America would never again be governed by any human monarch.

The nation that had been colonized out of a need for people to freely worship God in truth and spirit was taking the final step to secure that right. A method of worship that Jesus had told the Samaritan woman would someday evolve, had come to pass. In declaring independence from England, America was, in essence, declaring that it would never again depend on an earthly king. From that fateful day, July 4, 1776, the founders of these United States of America took every precaution possible to ensure that no one man, indeed, that no one *group* of men, would hold absolute power over the people of the nation. The founders went so far as to establish three branches of government, and later, more than one political party to ensure the freedom that became so costly in those days following that July 4th declaration.

Increasingly, God would be woven into the fabric of America. Patriotic songs referenced God and became songs of praise as well as of patriotism. "God Bless America" demonstrates the abiding belief of Americans that their country and every good thing in it and about it is a gift from God. American money is imprinted with the words "In God We Trust," a constant reminder that, literally, America's fortune comes from God, as well as a constant warning against idolatry. Americans are not to worship money or the gold that backs the money, but God, who provides all.

God would become the guiding light and sole Ruler of the young nation; not by force, but by faith. In declaring independence from human kings, America was signaling her understanding that it made no sense to put faith in human authority. After all, human authority was what had driven the first American colonists out of Europe and in search for a place to freely worship God. From July 4, 1776, onward, Americans would choose to put their faith in God, not in man.

PRAYER

GOD and Father, we come to You on this day of national independence to declare once more our willing and universal dependence on You. We come before You today not only to ask: *God, Bless America*; but to declare with our hearts and minds and spirits: *America, let us Bless God.* God of our country, Creator of every country and every world and every living thing, we thank You today for the freedoms only You can give us: the freedom from tyranny; the freedom from idolatry; the freedom of truth; the freedom of faith, which brings us peace if only we seek it. Teach us to seek that peace and freedom inherent only in You, Lord. Remind us when we grow arrogant as a nation and as individuals that we are and have nothing without You. Curb any deceitful desire we might have to limit the freedoms of others in this nation and throughout the world. Let us always remember that we are to follow Jesus' example and wash, not bind, the feet of others. Let us use the great power You have given us for the good of all. As we celebrate this joyful anniversary in our nation's history, as we are thrilled by fireworks and sated by cookouts, lead us to share the bounty You have provided us with all who are in need. And let us show You to all who seek and need You in this country and in the world. Amen.

ACTIVITY

A MID all the excitement and activity today, create a time of quiet thanksgiving. If possible, stop at a church or another sacred place and spend time thanking God for the freedoms you enjoy and those who fought for them. Invite family members, friends, colleagues, or neighbors to join you in these moments of rejoicing and thanksgiving. Whether you are alone or with others, name the things you are thankful for. Consider how they are related to the freedoms we celebrate today. Think about or discuss ways to share these products of freedom with others. Finally, pray for those in this country and other countries who are not free.

HENRY DAVID THOREAU'S BIRTHDAY

IT is very difficult, some would say impossible, to live one's life according to one's highest ideals. Few of us manage to even come close. Life is so complicated. There are so many compromises that seem to be necessary along the way. We need to make a living. We need to "go along to get along." We need to win approval, get a good education so we can get a good job so we can marry and care for our families so we can be good daughters and sons to our elderly parents so we can . . . well, it all ends the same way. But quite often, along that way, we can forget what we really believe in, what our highest hopes for ourselves are or were.

It is rare to know someone who bucks that everlasting trend and hews close to what he or she holds most dear. It is even rarer for such a person to manage to be patriotic while living in such a pure fashion. Henry David Thoreau was just such a person. He was an American Original who managed to be true to his beliefs and his vision of what America stood for, even when America itself did not measure up to those high ideals.

Born on July 12, 1817, Thoreau is best known as a naturalist, speaker, author and poet, although these were perhaps just public expressions of the multifaceted man he became. His most famous works, *Walden*, which told of his two years and two months living alone in a cabin he built on Walden Pond; and "Civil Disobedience," his essay on the moral imperative for an individual to resist immoral government, have come to define him as a person apart from the world. Some might suggest, he lived apart from reality. However, Thoreau was intensely engaged in his world. He was perhaps the most ambitious kind of patriot in that he wanted the best from the great experiment of the United States of America and was ready to criticize anything less, writing in "Civil Disobedience": "I ask for, not at once no government, but at once a better government."

Over the years many people have made Henry David Thoreau into what they needed him to be, and because he managed to be so many things during his short life, such one-dimensionalizing of Thoreau has become common. He was firmly against slavery, and so to abolitionists, he was the model abolitionist. He left behind a 20-volume journal, and so to memoirists, he wrote the ultimate memoir. He practiced and wrote about civil disobedience, and so to men like Mahatma Gandhi and Martin Luther King, Jr., he was the original non-violent protester. He loved and wrote about nature, and so to ecologists, he was the premier environmentalist.

Yet, Henry David Thoreau, who died at the young age of 44 of tuberculosis in 1862, was uniquely himself. A contradiction at times, Thoreau could be both hermit and intimate friend, both observer and participant, both writer and speaker, both introverted and focused on achieving literary success, both motionless in nature and moving through it. Thoreau was also a man of deep faith, something not often cited in discussions about the writer. His deep love of nature was, for him, inextricably interwoven with his love of God; he once noted that he liked to gaze at the stars to see whether he could see God behind them. As his health failed, those around him were comforted by his calm readiness for death, and when his aunt asked him on his deathbed whether he had made peace with God, Henry replied, "I did not know we had ever quarreled."

Would that every one of us could have the same response when our time comes.

PRAYER

GOD in and from Whom is all nature and creation, we thank You for men and women like Henry David Thoreau. We praise

You for giving us models of how to live purely and according to our highest ideals, of how to seek You in nature, and of how to support Your laws in government. Help us to worry less about how people see us or what others think of us and more about staying true to You, Your commandments, and Your creation. Teach us to express ourselves with respect for all, but let us never compromise on those things we know are right and good for ourselves, our environment, and our country. Amen.

ACTIVITY

TODAY, in celebration of Henry David Thoreau's birthday, seek God in nature. Observe and enjoy. Try to find God behind the stars as Thoreau did. Take a long walk near a river or pond, through the woods or along a country road; or, if you live in a city, wander through a park paying attention to every living thing in it. Feel the warmth of God's sun on your face and body and note how its light strikes a blade of grass, the mica chips in a sidewalk, the petals of a rose. If God has given rain today, let it fall on your face. Watch it soak into the ground, giving life. Watch the sun rise or set even if it is an overcast day. Note how your feelings are tied to the weather and be grateful to God for this connection.

JULY 14

BLESSED KATERI TEKAKWITHA

IN discussions of saints and saints-to-be from the United States, Blessed Kateri Tekakwitha is often overlooked. And yet, she, unlike many U.S. saints, is truly an American. An *original* American. She is also one of the first in the New World to be named a "Blessed," having lived over a century before the United States of America actually existed. On October 21, 2012 she will be declared the first Native American Saint by Pope Benedict XVI.

Kateri Tekakwitha was born in 1656 near Auriesville, in what became the state of New York. She was born into the Mohawk Indian tribe, the daughter of a warrior. By the time she was four years old, her mother had died of smallpox, possibly a strain of the disease brought to the continent by European settlers. Kateri caught the disease from her mother, and though smallpox did not kill her, it scarred her face. After her mother's death, the child was adopted by relatives, but her suffering had just begun.

She converted to Christianity as a teenager, and as a result, was scorned by her own Native American people who believed that nothing good could come from the White people who had brought so much ill to their world.

Nevertheless, Kateri was baptized at the age of twenty and continued to persevere despite growing anger and bitter disdain from her tribe. Finally, she traveled to a new Christian colony of Native Americans in Canada where she lived out her young life caring for the ill and the older members of the community.

Known for her commitment to prayer and penance, Kateri was also extremely dedicated to the Holy Eucharist and to the crucified Jesus. It is believed that her great devotion to Jesus Crucified resulted from the depth of her own suffering in life. She is also remembered for braving even the harshest Canadian winters to wait outside the chapel door before dawn at 4 a.m. every morning for Mass, and she would remain in the chapel until after the last Mass was finished. Kateri Tekakwitha died in 1680 at only twenty-four years of age. No stranger to personal suffering himself, Pope John Paul II beatified her three hundred years after her death, and she is now called the Lily of the Mohawks.

Not only was Kateri Tekakwitha among the first of the Native People in America to be recognized by the Church and Christians worldwide, she is also a poignant reminder of how the grand experiment of America is not just one thing, but a sometimes tangled mixture—both great and not-so-great—of many things and many peoples. The same European settlers, many in search of a place where they could freely practice their faith, who brought disease and destruction to the Native American tribes, also helped sow the seeds of Christianity. Kateri experienced both great loss and greater gain through this, and it was her commitment to Christ that allowed her to bridge the gap between the New and Old Worlds; a gap in which was eventually formed the country we know today. As Americans of faith, we are not a pure-breed! We are inextricably tied to those who came before us, both Native People and settlers, both free and enslaved: and we are bound by those ties to follow the "greatest commandments" laid down by Jesus over 2,000 years ago: to love God with our entire selves and all our strength, and to love others as we love ourselves.

PRAYER

LORD, we thank You for the richness of America! We praise You for weaving so many traditions into the culture of the United States, a culture that continues to change and encompass all who come here. We thank You for the people who are native to this nation, for their contributions and for their deep and abiding respect for the land. Help us to learn from them, Lord, for they are a people who do not value ownership or the false cult of self, two aberrations that many Americans fall prey to. Teach us to honor their ways. Remind us that they worshiped You in their own traditions, even before they came to know You through Jesus Christ. Help us to remember always that Americans do not own America, that it is not "ours" to keep from others, but that this land where we live is Yours and Yours alone. You have given it to us to share, and remind us that this is our duty as Christians. Amen.

ACTIVITY

IN honor of Kateri Tekakwitha, do some research. Discover what Native People lived or traveled through your state. Learn about their culture. What did they eat? How did they clothe themselves? What were their traditions? Were they farmers? Hunters? Warriors? How did they perceive the land? How did they worship? Study their history. What happened to them when Europeans and others started to settle in America? Do any members of these tribes survive? Where are they now? Finally, ask yourself what you can do to honor their memory and/or those who remain. And then do it.

AUGUST 15

BLESSED ASSUMPTION

WHEN I was a child, I attended a Catholic elementary school. There were a number of life-sized statues of various saints, and, of course, of Jesus and Mary. The saints were, for the most part, rather somber looking, even forbidding in some cases. But the statue of Mary appeared friendly and gentle to my young eyes. Her arms were at her sides, though a little outstretched with the palms open as if about to welcome a child into her embrace. She had a small smile on her face and her eyes looked kindly out upon the hallway. Unlike the other saints, she seemed to be right at home in a school filled with children.

Moreover, she stood next to an American flag. It seemed natural to me that she should be there. When we said the Pledge of Allegiance, there she was, smiling in approval. When we uttered the words, "One nation, under God," she seemed delighted. When we put our small hands over our hearts, she seemed to cover ours with hers. So perhaps I can be forgiven for assuming that, just as I learned how George Washington was the father of our country, I naturally assumed that Mary was the mother of our country!

Obviously, I knew nothing then about the separation of church and state, or about the shiver of dismay some Americans would feel at my childish notion. Still, just as there was comfort for a shy, chubby first-grader in the statue of a sweet, loving Mary standing near the flag, so there can be comfort in the idea of Mary watching over us and our country as a mother would. Surely she would understand the feelings of a mother who puts aside her own comfort and well-being to send a beloved child to college or to help her start a business or him to buy a house. Mary would know the anxiety of a mother who watches her child march off to serve the nation and the world as a volunteer or a soldier. Mary would empathize with a mother who bites her tongue as her child goes down a path she would not choose for him or her. And Mary would most certainly feel the anguish of the mother who learns that her child is lost to her through death, addiction, or separation. In all these cases Mary would not care about the economic status, the race, the ethnicity of the mother and child. She would take no notice of their place in society, what kind of clothes they could afford, what they ate. She would care only for what they felt, what they did, what they suffered. Mary is God's gift of compassion, wrapped in flesh.

Indeed, for these reasons and many more, Mary is celebrated throughout North and South America and is considered Patroness of the Americas. Starting in Mexico, where the Shrine of Our Lady of Guadalupe is one of the most popular pilgrimage sites in North America, more and more believers came to identify with Mary as mother, patroness, protector. In Latin America, particularly, Mary is the one people turn to for help in any difficulty whether national, religious, or personal. In the United States many ethnic communities take advantage of the good summer weather to have parades and festivals on this day in Mary's honor. A number of processions through city and village streets feature a statue of Mary being carried aloft.

Every year on August 15, many Christians throughout the Americas and in the United States celebrate the day that Mary, having died, was taken—or assumed—into heaven. Though this miracle inspires amazement and awe in American Christians, it never stops us from turning to Mary for her gentle strength, compassion, and empathy in times of need.

So, maybe I wasn't so far off the mark as a six-year-old believing that Mary was our nation's mother. Can we really imagine a better one?

PRAYER

MARY, mother of God and our mother, take us, your adopted children, to your heart. Comfort us when we are sad and grieving. Guide us when we don't know what to do or how to do it. Pray for us when we need your prayers (always). Help us to turn to your example of love, sacrifice, selflessness, and compassion in our dealings with other people and other nations. Thank you for giving yourself as the means for God to be born into our world. Let us never forget that whatever we may feel or suffer, you understand. Amen.

ACTIVITY

TODAY, try to do as Mary would do. If you see someone who is sad or suffering, try to comfort that person. If someone in your life is heading in a negative direction, reach out to that person in a non-judgmental way. Be kind to a child. Do without something you want so that someone else may have it; in fact, if you can, give it away yourself, whether it is a piece of clothing, a sandwich or cup of coffee, a few dollars. Respect your spouse. Listen to your children. Guide them as lovingly as you can. Just don't expect them to turn water into wine: only Mary's Son could do that.

SAINT ELIZABETH ANN SETON'S BIRTHDAY

THE portrait of Elizabeth Ann Seton was in many ways that of the ideal American saint. Born on August 28, 1774, in Staten Island during the dawn of the Independence movement in this nation, she came from a family that might have been described as American nobility. Like many of the upper class Americans at the time, her family was Anglican and they most likely worshiped at the large and distinguished Trinity Church in New York. Elizabeth was raised as a strong Episcopalian and incorporated her faith into her daily life.

The advantages she was born with were soon tempered by suffering, sickness, and death. At the age of 20, she married William Seton, and though they had five children together, William was not well. His business ventures failed and the family was forced into bankruptcy. His illness worsened after they traveled to Italy to find a cure, and, although Elizabeth nursed him selflessly, he died there in 1803. They'd had barely a decade together. During their sojourn in Italy, Elizabeth learned more about Roman Catholicism and met many Roman Catholics. As a result, she joined the

Roman Catholic Church in 1805 not long after her husband's death.

Her conversion to Roman Catholicism gave Elizabeth the strength to go on in her grief and to transform her suffering into important work for the Church. Her family, however, was appalled at her conversion and added to her suffering by rejecting her. Despite being in continual financial difficulties, she was given an opportunity by a priest to advance the cause of Christianity in the young United States of America and Elizabeth pursued this opportunity diligently. Within a few years of her husband's death and her return to America, she had opened her first Catholic school in Baltimore in 1808.

A year later, she founded a religious community of teaching sisters called the Sisters of St. Joseph in Emmitsburg, Maryland. From this beginning, Mother Seton, as she came to be known, began to create schools throughout the region, eventually including New York, Ohio, Pennsylvania, New Jersey, and Missouri. She was responsible for spreading Catholicism and Catholic teaching throughout much of the American heartland. She died at the age of 46 and was made a saint over 150 years later in 1975. At the time of her death, her religious order, the first female order in the United States, had grown to over 20 communities.

Mother Seton represents the best of America and Christianity in her willingness to be extraordinarily generous with her own means while pursuing the American ideal of education for all children, regardless of their socio-economic status. She also overcame her own tragedy and sorrow by throwing herself into work that benefited both Christianity and her country. In addition, by establishing a teaching order of religious sisters, Mother Seton strengthened a faith-filled presence in America's cities and bolstered a tradition of religious education for urban children.

Elizabeth Seton, with her wealthy and privileged background, participated in a tradition of philanthropy in the United States that was just finding a foothold during her own lifetime. Even before she opened her first Catholic girl's school, she had founded the Society for the Relief of Poor Widows with Small Children in New York City. America's truly great families were great in more than mere wealth. They were great in *how* they shared their wealth and in the institutions and magnificent cultural facilities they established through their power and influence. Even those that are non-denominational or secular were created, and continue, to serve all Americans; some particularly target the poor and disadvantaged in what is an undeniably Christian tradition. We can see this philanthropic custom continue today in the Bill and Melissa Gates Foundation and the financial and social commitments of people like Oprah Winfrey and Warren Buffett.

PRAYER

GOD of all that is good, we thank You for Mother Elizabeth Ann Seton, a woman who overcame her own personal grief and trouble to serve as a beacon of progress and hope for an untold number of children and families. We ask You to "convert" more of the men and women of privilege in this nation to the Christian and American ideal of philanthropy, for in the end, You make it so that all philanthropy is, indeed, Christian in that it helps those in need. Touch our own hearts, too, Lord, so that we may realize how much You have given us, and thus, find it within ourselves to share more of Your gifts to us with others. Amen.

ACTIVITY

IN honor of Saint Elizabeth Ann Seton, take action to support education. Whether you choose to support Christian-based education or public education is not as important as getting involved in some form of teaching and learning. If you cannot afford even a small donation to an educational facility or school, then consider helping with a fund raiser. You can also volunteer at a local school or daycare center. Go to a drama or musical production offered by your local school system. Cheer on a local sports or debate or spelling team. Outside of traditional school-based programs, you may contribute to and/or volunteer for a literacy organization or your library.

SEPTEMBER—FIRST MONDAY

LABOR DAY

JUST in case the irony of celebrating a holiday devoted to labor by having no one work is lost on us, a number of columnists and bloggers will surely remind us each year as Labor Day approaches. But the origins of this American holiday are far from lighthearted, and the fact that Labor Day today is seen as little more than "the last long weekend of summer," is troubling to those who believe that workers, especially workers' unions and workers' rights, are central to the health of America.

The concept of setting aside a day to honor America's workers, those we would today call blue collar workers, is over 125 years old. There is an ongoing disagreement about who first proposed Labor Day. The choice is between two men who headed up the most powerful unions in the country long before they united. Some believe that Peter J. McGuire, a member of the American Federation of Labor, first suggested that the United States follow Toronto, Canada's lead in creating an annual labor festival. Others say that a Labor Day was first proposed by machinist, Matthew Maguire, while he was secretary of the Central Labor Union of New York. The fact that the two labor leaders had similar names and that they both called for the national holiday in 1882 only muddles the question of who was first.

Oregon first declared Labor Day a state holiday in 1887, followed by 30 other states before it became a federal holiday in 1894. But the circumstances under which the festival became a holiday were far from festive and more about appeasing laborers than honoring them. During the 1894 strike of Pullman workers, a number of the strikers were killed by United States military personnel and United States Marshals who were called out by the government against the strikers. President Grover Cleveland, eager to end the strike and the bloodshed, worked out a deal and reconciled with the Labor movement. Congress, fearing the fallout from the strike, was not far behind. A mere six days after the strike ended, legislation establishing a national holiday had sped through Congress, and President Cleveland signed it into law.

Even at that point, controversy attended the process. President Cleveland insisted that the holiday be celebrated in September as had become the custom of the Central Labor Union of New York and other trade unions throughout the United States. The President and Congress were worried that laborers might push for making the American Labor Day coincide with an

International Worker's Day, in a gesture that could be perceived as showing solidarity with the newly born international Communist movement. As it was, and has been, while the Labor movement in the United States certainly flirted with socialism and communism, it increasingly came down on the side of labor being a pillar, and not an opponent, of capitalism.

Those who are anxious that Labor Day not fade into an end-of-summer afterthought are the same Americans who believe that our country was built on an ethic of hard work and adequately rewarding those who do it. The growing chasm between America's traditional workers and its extremely wealthy is of great concern. Some fear that we will lose our sense of the dignity and the efficacy of work in an age where those who produce nothing tangible in the way of goods and services are lavishly rewarded while the average working family struggles to stay solvent. For those Americans who identify with the hard workers of the New Testament like Jesus and Joseph, and Peter, John and James, the fishermen, Labor Day has become a somewhat bittersweet holiday in America.

PRAYER

JESUS, carpenter, teacher, and itinerant preacher, You worked hard every day of Your life. You surrounded Yourself with men and women who knew the dignity and necessity of physical work. You brought Your message to those who lived more often in tents and huts than in palaces and temples. Lord, when we are overwhelmed, worried about, or just plain bored, by our work, encourage us. Grant us the patience and the skill to do our jobs well. When we are anxious about our work, ease our minds and secure our positions. When we are unemployed or underemployed, lead us to the kind of employment that will provide dignity and sustenance. Help us to always speak out for workers in this country and throughout the world. Amen.

ACTIVITY

TOMORROW (since not that many people will be working today!), make an effort to treat every worker you encounter with an extra measure of respect and decency. From your spouse, who may be working either in your home or outside it, to the person who gets you your coffee and muffin, to the receptionist or secretary at your workplace, to the cook at the cafe who prepares your lunch, to the teller at your bank, to the cashier at the grocery store, to the person who pumps your gas . . . be sure to say a kind word, drop a compliment, leave a tip, or even comment on the weather. And as you move onto the next thing in your day, don't forget to say, "God Bless you!"

9/11 REMEMBRANCE DAY

A S I write this, it is 9/10/11, the eve of the tenth anniversary of what we've come to know in America as simply 9/11. Of course, there was nothing simple about it. The September 11, 2001 terrorist attack on this country that took so many lives, including the lives of many who survived that terrible day, shook the United States of America to its very core. Never before had an enemy successfully attacked mainland America. Never before had Americans of all races and religions been murdered and devastated in their own workplaces, homes, and travels during what we all thought was "peacetime." We Americans, in our confidence and power, had not conceived of the images that we saw that day, images branded on our collective and individual consciousness forever after. In the days and weeks following 9/11, so many said the words, "We will never be the same again."

As I write, magazines and newspapers, blogs and web sites, television and radio programs are all focused on the anniversary and, to an extent, that very question. I've noticed that a number of the articles and programs are looking at how America survived and moved forward. Stories are describing families who have never forgotten their lost loved ones, but have tried to honor their memories by choosing hope and progress and peace. I read about a woman who lost her husband of decades and decided to devote her life to promoting tolerance and peace, even testifying for the defense at a trial for one of the terrorists. *People* magazine's cover piece centers on "the children of 9/11," describing stories of perseverance and hope. *The Boston Globe's* front page highlights a college student who lost his father, who'd also been his best friend, and is now poignantly reliving their relationship as he watches his own year-old son discover the world around him.

The truth is that as a country and individuals we will never be the same, and we haven't fully recovered. How could it be otherwise? And yet in certain cases, we have made some progress away from grief and toward hope. Away from ignorance and toward information. Away from arrogance and toward understanding. And in the best cases, away from self-absorption and toward God.

Shortly after the attacks, I saw a church post a new combination of an old prayer on its outdoor signboard: **America Bless God.** How often do we say (and even sing!) the words "God Bless America," with pride and righteousness, even a sense of entitlement? It can sometimes sound like a demand, rather than a prayer. The lesson for God's people in the United States is that God's blessing is not something automatically due to us because we live in a great and powerful country. Yes, God has, does, and we pray, will always, bless America. But I think the point of that church board was that God does not bless a political or economic entity, nor does He stamp with approval all the things we do as a nation. Like any nation, we have done good and we have done harm. It seems ridiculous to believe that God blesses the harm we do, as individuals or as a country.

As God's people in the most powerful nation on earth, it is our job to bless and praise God; to ask for His help and direction, to give thanks when we get it right and to ask for forgiveness when we don't. And, as 9/11 reminds us, we must be a humble, grateful nation, never neglecting to ask for His protection.

PRAYER

GOD of power and might, we confess that we at times forget that we are nothing without You. For what does political power signify in the face of Your glorious power? What does economic prosperity mean to the One in Whom all riches find their source? What does military strength matter to You Who sent Your Son to counsel peace and love of all? What do national and political boundaries look like to the One Who made the whole earth and universe? Forgive us, Lord, for the times we forget how puny and dependent we are on Your grace and love. Protect us from others and from our own arrogance and human power. Teach us to do the hardest things: to practice humility and to love our enemies. And when we fail, remind us gently to try again. Amen.

ACTIVITY

DO something today to advance peace and healing. Write and send a kind note to someone who suffered a loss on 9/11. Read Gospel accounts of Jesus urging us to love our enemies, and our neighbors as ourselves. Read scripture passages from the Torah and the Koran. Send a contribution to UNICEF, Heifer International, Americares, Ox-Fam, Doctors Without Borders, FINCA, or another non-profit organization that helps hurting people internationally. Write a letter to your congressperson or senator expressing your thoughts about how America has changed in the decade since the terrorist attacks. Go to a church. Pray for God to grant you peace. Ask Him to grant peace to all troubled and confused people in the world.

Ask God to bless those who are open to a peace, not necessarily of calmness, harmony, and tranquility, but a peace that transcends the circumstances of their life; a peace that is beyond all comprehension.

Blessed are those who are persecuted for righteousness' sake, for theirs is the kingdom of heaven. *(Mt 5:10)*

Blessed be those who love God more than peace itself. Blessed be those who are willing to risk opposition, hostility, and rejection in order to listen to the voice of their heart, and march to the beat of the heavenly drum.

Blessed be those who are willing to lose that which is precious to them, in order to preserve that which is the most precious.

Blessed be those who are willing to sacrifice in the name of love, for theirs is the joy of courage.

Your healing peace is ours, dear God, even in the midst of the tempest. As we stay true to our belief and live according to your will, Beloved, we may encounter opposition. But whatever suffering may come our way, it cannot touch us at the core where you abide.

SEPTEMBER 17

UNITED STATES CONSTITUTION SIGNED BY MEMBERS OF THE CONVENTION

ON September 17, 1787, something happened in the New World that changed the whole world. More accurately described, the event was the culmination of years of war, debates, compromises, and the combination of bits and pieces from religion and philosophy that coalesced into something truly revolutionary. When 39 men signed The Constitution of the United States of America, they created a new thing in the world: the blueprint for a working national government that manifested the concept of democracy. These United States were, in theory and practice, intended to be a nation governed by the people through representatives they elected.

Such a thing was unheard of in the history of successful nation-states. The rest of the world might have laughed had it not just witnessed the effective defeat of Great Britain at the hands of its upstart former colony. But even if the world didn't laugh out loud, it surely believed that the United States of America was an arrogant construct that would go down in flames.

It didn't.

On the other hand, it has been and continues to be both a great and a messy experiment. Much has been made of the short introduction to the Constitution: *We the People of the United States, in order to form a more perfect Union, establish Justice, insure domestic Tranquillity, provide for the common defense, promote the general Welfare, and secure the Blessings of Liberty to ourselves and our Posterity, do ordain and establish this Constitution of America.*

As is often done with the Bible, people interpret these words, and the articles of government that follow, in ways that suit them and their various agendas. Politicians gleefully quote parts of the constitution—sometimes mistakenly—to support one position, while ignoring another part of the document that may not be so friendly to that position. Yes, there is something in the Constitution for just about everyone, particularly when taking into account the amendments added over the years.

For instance, the first amendment offers 16 words that continue to cause discord today: *Congress shall make no law respecting an establishment of religion, or prohibiting the free exercise thereof.* These words have been used by everyone from church leaders who say they should not have to pay taxes to atheists who oppose Christmas mangers on the public green.

How could there be so much contention over a document meant to form a more perfect union and establish justice and tranquillity? Quite easily, as it turned out, because it is in the nature of the document—and the country— to give every citizen a stake in America. And if everyone has a stake, everyone will have opinions about what the words establishing that stake should mean.

Sounds like a recipe for disaster, right? Yet, it isn't. The Constitution—literally: the framework of the country is founded on a spirit of struggle, a spirit that seeks to do the seemingly impossible: include all of the governed in the government. Christians undergo the same struggle. The Constitution of the Body of Christ in the world must, by its nature and Jesus' teachings, seek to include and recognize the inherent worth of all members, and, in fact, those who may not yet be members. This spirit of inclusion can and has caused all manner of dissent as various people and sects settle on various interpretations and positions. In both cases, that of Christianity and that of America—human nature is hard at work!

But just as the reality of contention among the governed and the governors of America cannot change the ambitious, revolutionary spirit of the Constitution, so is the spirit of Christianity as Jesus established it unchanged by the human debate.

PRAYER

LORD and Governor of all the worlds, help us to live first according to the Body of Christ in the world and then according to our national Constitution. Let us never become complacent in either our efforts to do God's will as taught by Jesus Christ or in our struggle to make America adhere to the greatness its early leaders aspired to in drafting the Constitution. Help us to avoid the distractions of pettiness, destructive competition, and angry debate as we seek to fulfill the promise of the Spirit and pursue the spirit of democracy. In both our churches and our seats of government, let us shun corruption, fraud, deceit, and selfishness. Help us to demonstrate in our lives, words and works, our commitment to God and country. Amen.

ACTIVITY

OBTAIN a copy of the Constitution of the United States of America today and read it either by yourself or with others. Carefully read the entire constitution including the amendments. Marvel at how short and concise a document established such a large, sprawling nation. Try to put aside any political convictions, prejudices, and opinions on government that you might hold as you read. Make an effort to read it "fresh" as though you were reading in 1787 when the concept of a democratic nation was profoundly radical. Note the care that went into establishing the branches of government, their powers and responsibilities, their limits. Consider the ways in which America has fulfilled the vision of its Constitution and the ways in which we have failed thus far. If you are reading with others, discuss these points. Ask yourself and each other what you can do, as Christians, to promote a more perfect union. Ask God to help you do it.

EMANCIPATION PROCLAMATION

CONSIDERED one of the most important executive orders ever issued by an American President, the Emancipation Proclamation actually was a two-part declaration made by President Abraham Lincoln during the American Civil War. On September 22, 1862, Lincoln issued the first executive order, or part one, of the Emancipation Proclamation, declaring the freedom of all slaves in the southern, or Confederate, states. The second executive order was issued on January 1, 1863, specifically naming the states where slaves were declared freed and setting off a firestorm of criticism since the states named were the very states that had seceded from the Union and therefore claimed that Lincoln had no power over them. They recognized their own President, Jefferson Davis. Of course, slavery continued to exist, even legally, in some parts of the United States until enough states ratified the Thirteenth Amendment to the Constitution on December 18, 1865, officially ending all legal slavery in the country.

Today we take it for granted that President Lincoln had the power to issue the Emancipation Proclamation; indeed, some wonder why he waited so long. But at the time, the United

States was still a relatively young and untested union and the powers designated by the Constitution were open to debate, or at the very least, interpretation. The President's powers were extremely limited by the founding fathers, who, having just defeated the English king, greatly distrusted the notion of too much power in the hands of a Chief Executive, even a duly elected one.

In the end Lincoln justified his power to issue the proclamation by citing Article II, section 2 of the United States Constitution which gives the President the power to be "Commander and Chief of the Army and Navy of the United States, and of the Militia of the several States, when called into the actual Service of the United States." This was the only line in the Constitution that irrevocably gave Lincoln the power to issue the Emancipation Proclamation, and there is some question about whether he could have legally done it were the country not at war.

As with most issues involving the Civil War, there is still a debate about whether Lincoln issued the Emancipation Proclamation primarily to end slavery or as a part of the Union's war strategy. Once the first part of the proclamation was ordered, many slaves redoubled their efforts to escape into the Union and join the fight against their former owners. So, was the Emancipation Proclamation a shining beacon of freedom from a country that stood for the ideal, or was it a thinly veiled attempt to demoralize and out-man the Confederacy?

Probably both, history tells us, but as Christians, we wonder: does it really matter? The result was that men and women who had been torn from their homes, dragged to this country in chains, separated from their spouses and children, and forced to work with fewer rights than animals, were finally recognized as free human beings. No matter how cynical we are, there is great power in the law; and in issuing the Proclamation, Lincoln was reversing centuries of practice in America by making it illegal to own another human being. He was announcing to all the world that our country had been irrefutably wrong to build its prosperity on the backs of people who had no opportunity to partake in it freely. The Emancipation Proclamation was confession and repentance all rolled into one glorious declaration. Lincoln was ensuring that the law of the United States would finally reflect the law of God.

PRAYER

JESUS, You came to our world to free it, and us. We would no longer be slaves to sin, but sons and daughters of the Father. Lord,

You came to free all of us, not just those who held and hold power and wealth. Yet, for too many years in our nation, even before it was a nation, people from Africa and the Caribbean were slaves to the sins of America. They were bound, through no fault of their own, to the sins of greed, power, and slavery. We praise You, Lord, for giving Abraham Lincoln the strength and courage to free them and our nation from this depraved captivity. We ask You to empower us, as a nation and as individuals, to stand against slavery anywhere it exists and in any form it still takes. Help us to build a world where everyone chooses to serve only one master: You. Amen.

ACTIVITY

THINK of a place or a way in which slavery still exists in our world. We hear news stories of people being stolen or lured into sex slavery and domestic servitude. We understand that people are enslaved by addiction. We may know people who, because of abusive or traumatic childhoods, are bound up in relationships or situations that are degrading and inhuman. Extreme poverty can strip people of all dignity and self-esteem, forcing them into the kind of slavery that may cause them to sell themselves or even surrender their lives to try to escape. We've read of desperate immigrants who will do anything to flee poverty and terrorism in their own countries. Do something to address one of these situations. Learn more. Volunteer for an organization that helps people in such tragic circumstances. Donate time and money. Pray for all who are enslaved and ask God to show you how to help.

SEPTEMBER 23

FIRST DAY OF AUTUMN

THE first day of Autumn, like the season itself, is a bit fickle. Some years it falls on September 22, others on September 23. Some years it is hot with abundant sunshine in a forceful imitation of the summer we are leaving behind, others it is rainy and cold in advance of the winter we will soon experience. The exact date, actually the exact moment of the autumnal equinox, is determined astronomically according to the time that the sun passes directly over the earth's equator and the earth is tilted neither away nor toward the sun. Consequently, the 24-hour period at this point will be just about evenly divided between light, or day, and darkness, or night. The actual moment that the sun crosses the equator is measured, defined, and noted by the International Astronomical Union.

For many North Americans—especially those in northern climates—the first day of autumn is a somewhat bittersweet day. While the weather is usually still good and there's enough daylight to get lots done and spend time outside, September 22 or 23 represents the long, quickening slide toward winter. The crisp apples and luscious pears that are fresh off the trees now will soon be stored for the long, fruitless season to come. The harvest of spring and summer provide a bounty that almost makes us forget what it will be like in a few months when the farmers' markets are closed and the choices for fresh food dwindle. The brilliant colors of the leaves that are just starting to turn provide the deceptively lovely raiment to what will soon appear as barren and dry tree limbs, rattling in the cold wind. The few patches of dried-up grass are a reminder of how the green lawns and fields will soon be replaced with brown and gray and, finally, white. That first nip in the air makes us think of calling the oil company to insure we will have enough fuel to keep our furnaces going for the next six or seven months.

All but the most committed skiers and snow boarders would probably like to hold onto summer just a little bit longer. And for quite a few more days, if not weeks, we'll be able to do just that with occasionally warm and bright days that will almost convince us that autumn might last forever this year and never plummet into the void of winter. On particularly warm days in October, it becomes even easier to be lulled into a false sense of security. Winter, however, is inevitable.

And yet, God, Who gives us everything in due season, also always gives us a little something to hold onto. There is a small roadside patch along my daily walk; it is weedy with scant grass even during the halcyon days of summer. It's not even part of anyone's yard. Nothing much to look at. But every September, usually around today, something amazing happens on that scraggly little patch. Crocuses bloom. Yes, the earliest flower of Spring, often showing up even before the snow is melted and disappearing long before the first really warm day, blooms at the beginning of Autumn on this pathetic little roadside stretch. In all their royal purple glory, the cheerful flowers raise their faces trustingly to the graying sky and foggy nights along the New London coast.

Autumn is a time to trust God. Of course, it's always time to trust God. He never leaves us without hope if only we have the courage to look for it.

PRAYER

G OD of surprises, Lord of hope, as we enter the season of Autumn, give us the grace to see all the good You have provided us in this, and every, season. We give You thanks for the agricultural products yielded over the past months and we look forward to what the earth will give us over the next weeks. We rejoice in the tastes and smells and beauty of this season. We praise You for reminding us that we are a nation founded on agriculture and blessed with abundant natural resources. Help us to avoid complacency and waste as we reap the bounty that You have sown. If we become anxious about the coming days of darkness and difficult weather, comfort us in the knowledge that You will never leave us alone. Amen.

ACTIVITY

AUTUMN usually signals a slowing down, a withdrawal, a time to step back from the busyness of Spring and Summer. Although your schedule may seem as frantic as ever, take time today or this week to acknowledge and enjoy this season of gradual retreat. Visit a roadside farmstand or even a working farm. Walk through a corn maze. Buy fresh fruit and vegetables. Try them in a new—or old—recipe. Carve a pumpkin and roast the seeds to save for winter. Take a sightseeing drive and try to spot the first signs of leaves turning on the trees. Buy corn candy or caramel apples. Relax with a book and warm apple cider. Take the time to savor God's gift of Autumn in America.

OCTOBER—SECOND MONDAY

COLUMBUS DAY

WHEN I was a child, one of the most exciting things about Columbus Day was that it would mark the first appearance of corn candy in the grocery stores. Not to mention fresh apple cider at harvest farm stands along rural roads. The rather sad fact that these decidedly inferior events were what we paid attention to—in addition to the fact that it was the first long weekend since the start of the school year—demonstrates how much we tend to take poor, old Christopher Columbus for granted.

Perhaps it had something to do with that vague sense of betrayal we all felt after being told by our parents that Christopher Columbus "discovered" America, only to learn in school that Leif Ericson had been here first. That was a mild version of the disappointment in learning that there is no Santa Claus, after all. Then later, as our social justice sensibilities kicked in, we grew annoyed with Columbus as we asked, "And what about the Native Americans??"

But Christopher Columbus wasn't always a slightly tarnished, taken-for-granted personage in America. In fact, since the late 1700s, he has been feted as quite a hero and not only in the United States. A number of countries in the Americas celebrate the anniversary of Columbus blundering onto the American continent on October 12, 1492. Several Latin American countries mark the holiday as *Dia de la Raza*; in the Bahamas, they celebrate Discovery Day; and in Uruguay it is called *Dia de las Americas*. Despite having lost over the years much of the territory Columbus gained for them, Spain still celebrates October 12 as *Dia de la Hispanidad* and *Fiesta Nacional*.

In the United States it was not, as may be presumed, an East Coast state that first honored Columbus landing on its shores. Colorado was the first state to declare Columbus Day an official state holiday in 1906, and it became a federal holiday in 1937. But by then Americans had been celebrating some form of Columbus Day for over 150 years with festivals in 1792 in New York and other U.S. cities marking the 300th anniversary of Columbus landing in the "New World." One hundred years later in 1892, President Benjamin Harrison asked American citizens to mark Columbus Day on the four hundredth anniversary of the intrepid sailor setting foot on the continent. It was during the 1892 celebration that a number of U.S. writers, politicians, teachers, and preachers began to more strongly tie the holiday to the traditions of patriotism and loyalty.

Two groups of Americans still hold a special place in their hearts for Christopher Columbus: Italians and Catholics; although perhaps given their affinity, it is more accurate to say they form one group. Because a great number of 19th century and early 20th century immigrants to America were Catholic and experienced intense discrimination, they formed organizations to defend themselves economically, socially, and politically. One of these was the Knights of Columbus, a Catholic group that chose Christopher Columbus as its namesake to remind Catholic persecutors that the "founder" of America had been a Catholic and an Italian. As a result of lobbying by the Knights of Columbus, President Franklin Delano Roosevelt established October 12 as an official federal holiday in 1934. In 1971 the holiday was moved to the second Monday in October, coinciding with Thanksgiving Day in Canada.

PRAYER

FATHER, the United States of America is often called a "melting pot" of people from different countries and cultures. Whether we were "discovered" by Columbus or Ericson or Native Americans, whether we were colonized by Great Britain or France or Spain, whether our religions were Catholic, Protestant,

Jewish, Muslim, or Indigenous . . . we are now so much more under Your loving watch. Help us to celebrate what unites us as a nation, and to accept our differences as individuals. Free us from the divisiveness of extremism, exclusion, and political grandstanding. Show us what Your will is for us as a nation, as families, as individuals; and give us the courage to follow You in all things. Amen.

ACTIVITY

CONSIDER the traditions you observe at this time of year. Maybe you're not a fan of corn candy, but do you decorate your home with Fall colors and materials? Do you visit farm stands for fresh apples, pears, or pumpkins? Do you take an annual ride to see "the colors" of Autumn? Do you watch for the first frost to take in your more delicate flowers and vegetable plants? Do you buy chrysanthemums for your table or to replace the wilting summer plants on your porch? Do you brew hot tea with lemon or sticks of cinnamon? Whatever your "Columbus Day" traditions may be, remind yourself as you observe them that they have come to exist because you live in a unique and vastly blessed country that has incorporated traditions and rituals from just about every corner of the earth into its own wondrous tapestry.

OCTOBER 24
UNITED NATIONS DAY

AT the end of World War II, the United States, and the entire world, was still reeling from the horrors of a war that perpetrated one of the most brutal genocides ever known to humankind, saw the consolidation of communism, was the beginning of the end of colonialism, and caused sorrow and loss in just about every country of the world. World War II literally changed the world, destroying whatever fragile sense of security people had after the end of World War I that there would be no more war on such a massive scale. World War II had literally redistributed power, marginalizing and weakening the empire of Great Britain, destroying the frightening military capacities of Germany and Japan, affirming the power of the United States, and establishing the Soviet Union, and then China, as the greatest threats to democracy in the world. In addition to all that, World War II ended with the nightmare of the atom bomb and the resulting race for nuclear supremacy.

Just about every nation on earth was shaken and made painfully aware of its altered place in the suddenly unstable sphere of global politics. Although the war was over, the peace promised to be an uncertain one with Stalin on the rise, Japan's and Germany's economies and major cities destroyed, and Europe divided into east and west.

The United Nations, which had come into existence after World War I to *prevent* just such another devastating occurrence, was in a strange and uncomfortable position at the end of World War II. Was it even relevant anymore? What could it achieve in a post-war world where power had been essentially divided between two massive countries now at enmity? Perhaps to answer that question as strongly and positively as possible, in 1947 the United Nations General Assembly proclaimed October 24, the original date of the founding Charter of the United Nations, as a day to be "devoted to making known to the peoples of the world the aims and achievements of the United Nations and to gaining their support for" the work of the organization.

To demonstrate its ambition and hope for unity and collaboration among the "peoples of the world," the United Nations General Assembly in 1971 issued an additional proc-lamation naming October 24, United Nations Day, as an international holiday and urging all member nations to observe it as a public holi-day. Throughout the world, and in the United States where the United Nations is based in

Manhattan, United Nations day and week (from October 20 to 26) are observed with meetings, events, exhibits, and programs highlighting the accomplishments and objectives of the organization. Worldwide, and especially at international schools, this is also a day or week to offer events, cultural and artistic performances, and food fairs showing off the diversity of their students and curricula. In America, the President traditionally issues a proclamation on October 24, celebrating the United Nations and the United States as its host country.

For American Christians the United Nations is a powerful symbol of unity. Although every member nation may not be primarily Christian, the commitment of the member nations to work together toward the greater good of the world mirrors the Christian commitment to work together with all of creation to fulfill God's will. Jesus instructed us to love all men and women, and to lead by example not by force. Empathy and compassion are vital tools of worldwide Christianity, just as they are key to producing global peace, stability, and prosperity.

PRAYER

LOVING God, thank You for giving humankind the motivation to come together to work on its problems and issues.

We praise You for giving men and women the impulse to implement such an ambitious strategy. We glorify You for giving us the strength to move forward with this objective in the face of seemingly great obstacles. Remind us that with You, nothing is impossible when we seek to do what is right in Your sight. Strengthen us in these challenging times to continue to progress with Your agenda of cooperation and unity. We rejoice in every step we take toward peace and prosperity for all Your children, wherever and whoever they may be. Amen.

ACTIVITY

SELECT a United Nations member country about which you know very little. Do some research on this country. What language do most of the people speak? What is their economy based upon? What religions are practiced there? How many people live there? What is the literacy rate? What is the average life expectancy of the people? What kind of foods do they eat? What are their traditions and holidays? What is their climate like? Make notes on all of these. Sketch, cut out or copy a picture of the country's flag and attach it to your notes. Look at this from time to time to remind yourself of your connection to this new friend-nation.

ANNIVERSARY OF THE
STOCK MARKET CRASH OF 1929

THE anniversary of the 1929 stock market crash is a little too close for comfort for many Americans today. Not necessarily in years; it happened almost a century ago. Several generations of Americans don't even remember it. But we feel the cold tendrils of national and family memory as we still struggle to recover from our own more recent near-depression. Indeed, many look to those dark days more than 82 years ago for some clues as to how to survive our current economic tempest. There has probably been more written about the Great Depression that officially began with the stock market plummeting on October 29, 1929, in the past five years than in the previous 50 as America—and the world—look for a way out of our present crisis.

Although the historical market crash occurred on October 29, 1929, it was not until three years later that the market actually hit its lowest point during the depression. Economists and investors today note that three years after the U.S. national crisis in the Fall of 2008 that triggered a difficult worldwide recession, the market is still in peril. And it is not only big investors who are affected. Millions of people have lost their jobs and still can't find new ones. People who have relied on modest equity growth from their homes have found themselves with property worth less than its mortgage. Older Americans who'd looked forward to a peaceful retirement are forced to postpone those plans indefinitely. Just as was the case during the 1930s, our national economic recovery looks to be a long, painful process.

For some Americans then, as well as today, desperation can become despair in an instant. Even those who didn't live through Black Tuesday in 1929 have seen images or read descriptions of investors who lost everything and committed suicide. It was not only the loss of wealth that drove them, but the humiliation and shame of having achieved a perceived status for themselves and their families only to see it vanish in what must have seemed like a heartbeat.

It is easy to ask, "Why me?" And though we may tell ourselves we are asking this of our elected leaders, economists, corporate chief executives, bankers and all the others we think should have answers but don't, the truth is that, in our hearts, we are crying this anguished question out to God. We want to know, as Job wanted to know, how God could have let such a thing happen to us, to America.

Fortunately for us, the God Who warned us against putting our trust in money, our faith in riches, our love into wealth, is a compassionate God. He may not answer our cry in the precise way we wish to be answered. He may not give us the explanations we so heartily desire. He may not restore our lost wealth the way we want it restored. He may not return our country to its previous level of financial prosperity. But if we seek Him, He will remain with us as we struggle and suffer. If we take His hand, He will guide us through our fear. If we open our hearts, He will feel our pain. And if we ask Him the right questions, He will teach us what we can learn from our mistakes.

PRAYER

FATHER, You cautioned us against the power and allure of wealth. You emblazoned Your commandments on a simple rock while the Israelites danced around a golden calf. You sent Your prophets into the desert with little more than the clothes they wore and strong voices. Your Son gave us parable after parable about the danger of wealth. And yet, Lord, money is a part of our world, a seeming necessity. Teach us how to use it. Guide our relationship with it. Help us to be generous with it. Prevent us from elevating it to a level that puts everything else in life in its shadow. Protect us from greed. When we become too confident in ourselves and our resources, remind us that everything we have comes from You. Amen.

ACTIVITY

MAKE a list of the ways in which our nation's economic troubles have negatively impacted you. Write down what you and your family have lost in terms of money, property values, employment, advancement opportunities, savings, and future plans. If you can no longer afford certain private schools or colleges for your children, include this on the list. If you can no longer provide for your parents or relatives the way you'd intended to, add this. Study the list and consider how these losses can bring you closer to God and to those you love. Can you use the challenges presented by the economic crisis to rely more faithfully on God? To pray more? To spend more time at church or volunteering? Can you give more of yourself to your family? Do you have the time to teach your children or help them with homework? If you have less money for restaurants and prepared meals, can you start to cook healthier food at home? Should you drive less and walk or bike more? Are these fearful times providing you with an opportunity to work on increasing your faith in God?

HALLOWEEN

WHEN we think of "modern-day" Halloween, with its elaborate parties and trick-or-treating for children and adults, its toilet-papered trees and smashed pumpkins, its sugary consequences of hyper kids and stomachaches, and its twilit parades and costume contests, we can easily forget that the origins of Halloween were decidedly religious.

The celebration of Halloween combines Catholic rituals, ancient Celtic beliefs, and parts of the Roman Empire's religious carnival called Feralia. All of these religious traditions chose the Fall, a time when warm daylight has faded and the cool darkness is more prevalent, to remember and, in some cases, to try to appease or escape those who have died. Superstitions and folk traditions from all over first century Europe naturally grew around such festivals, including an antiquated notion that the dead could walk the earth during this one night every year. The Celts would dress in costumes and light bonfires on Halloween to fool or scare off any lingering or malevolent spirits. In some Latino countries, people parade through cemeteries and visit graves to leave peace offerings so that the dead will not disturb the living.

It is a strange holiday in that it tries to rob, or even mock, death. Most religions are at least partially concerned with questions about death. What happens when we die? Will we be rewarded? Punished? Where will we go? How will we look? Will we recognize others or be recognized by them? Halloween, in a way, is an effort by humans to address these questions in a way that is not too threatening. It is a night when we try both to comfort ourselves about death by laughing at it or "trick or treating" it, while also scaring ourselves about it by entertaining superstitions and beliefs that may reflect our hidden fears.

Yet for people of faith in America, Halloween is increasingly becoming what it should be: a frivolous harvest festival where children get to wear scary masks and eat themselves silly. We need not, and should not, fear death, because we believe that death is the door to a new life with God. But for most of us, that fear lingers on even in the face of our faith. Very few people, outside of saints, find themselves ready to welcome death with open arms. It is natural to want to hold onto life with both hands, and to live it fully. It is natural, even, to want to laugh bravely in the face of death. Halloween gives us the opportunity to do just that, all the while realizing that our courage is founded in God.

PRAYER

GOD of the living and the dead, You alone understand the mysteries of death and life. You alone have the answers we seek and yet fear to know. You alone are able to turn the grief at death into the joy at new life. Guide us tonight and always as we struggle with these questions. Teach us to recognize the difference between fun and fear, between faith and superstition. Keep us safe and strengthen our faith as we try to understand Your will for us in life and in death. Help us to laugh in the face of death with our confidence placed firmly in You. Amen.

ACTIVITY

THERE is only one Spirit that matters and that is God's Spirit. Today, make an effort to assume for yourself one aspect of God's Spirit. Let that aspect be your Halloween "costume." If you wish to assume the aspect of compassion, go out of your way to show someone kindness in some tangible way. If you choose the aspect of forgiveness, then forgive an individual you've been holding something against, and make sure they know you've forgiven them. Or, seek forgiveness from someone you've wronged. If you choose generosity, do a good deed for someone in evident need. The list goes on. Choose your Halloween costume wisely . . . and consider wearing it again tomorrow.

NOVEMBER 1

ALL SAINTS' DAY

AS a child attending a Catholic elementary school, it didn't seem too strange to me that on the morning after we traipsed up and down our neighborhood streets, decked out in usually homemade costumes and seeking candy and other treats, we filed into Church, somberly dressed in our dark school uniforms for a Mass commemorating all the dead Saints. In fact, it seemed sort of fitting, since many of us had had our Halloween costumes "chosen" for us, and thus, we sought our treats dressed as either the Virgin Mary, an angel, or some popular saint. It was only as I grew up and began to attend public school, that I realized that not every little girl went out on Halloween dressed as Saint Teresa or Saint Veronica!

As an adult I wondered why the Church selected this particular day, following so close on the heels of an eve of goblins and monsters and vampires, to celebrate all of its saints. As it turns out, November 1 was not the original date for this celebration which dates back to over 1,400 years ago and probably even longer.

In the seventh century, the Roman emperor, Phocas, in recognition of the ascendancy of Christianity, gave the much celebrated Pantheon in Rome to Pope Boniface IV. Although historical records conflict on the actual date of the Pantheon's construction, it is generally believed to have been built by Marcus Agrippa during his third consulate in 27 B.C., although it is possible that the ancient temple existed long before that and that Agrippa merely restored and expanded the existing structure. It is believed that Agrippa dedicated the massive temple to Jupiter the Avenger, so it was a particular victory for Christianity when Phocas turned this symbol of the ancient gods over to the Catholic Church.

Pope Boniface IV, naturally committed to sealing and heightening this triumph, had the Pantheon converted into a church that he immediately consecrated to Mary, the Mother of God, and all the saints. The new church was formerly dedicated and the feast of this dedication was kept on May 13. Over a century later in 731, Pope Gregory III consecrated a chapel in St. Peter's Church for all the saints, and thereafter the feast of All Saints was celebrated in Rome. Another century passed and in 837, Pope Gregory IV was in France on the feast, and he encouraged that country to celebrate the festival. From there it spread throughout Europe and, eventually, to America.

In the United States we look to the saints as guides for our better selves, the agents of

Christianity in our country and in the world. Saints with origins in America have particularly represented the ideals, progressiveness, and mixed culture of this country. American saints tended to be driven, ambitious for Christianity, hardworking and dedicated to education and service. At the same time, they were people who did not easily "fit in" with their world, and they were often ready and willing to risk their social positions and reputations to pursue what they believed to be Christian objectives. They were, in a direct reflection of their country, independent.

PRAYER

FATHER of all saints and sinners, we thank You for the models of Christianity You give us in the saints, especially those who lived and worked in America. We praise You for their courage, strength, and discernment. We are grateful to You for sending Your energizing Spirit into these industrious men and women to help them overcome the considerable obstacles that were placed in their way. Help us to be like them, Lord! Encourage us in our pursuit of goodness and our commitment to help others. Strengthen us in our prayers and supplications. Lead us to do great things and to do them humbly in Your name. Amen.

ACTIVITY

DO you know any American saints? Not only through the pages of a book or a story or Church history, but through your own experience? In other words, do you know any real-live saints active and working in America today? You may have to think about it, but you probably do. There are many saint-like people among us, many of whom will never be recognized formally as saints, but who nonetheless love Jesus and do God's work. Consider the saints in your life. Your spouse perhaps (true in my case for the fact that he puts up with me!)? A teacher who manages even the most difficult children? A nurse or lab technician? The helpful cashier at your grocery store? The man who painted your house? A neighbor who gives away fresh fruit and vegetables from her abundant garden? Find a way to thank and recognize the saints in your life . . . and you may be on your way to becoming one of them.

ALL SOULS' DAY,
(DAY OF THE DEAD, MEXICO)

EVEN in modern-day America, we remain curious about death, and often feel deeply connected to those in our lives who have died, or at least to their memories. Though Christians in this country try to shun the superstitions and fears attending death and the loss of our departed loved ones and acquaintances, we still live with many questions and concerns about death and what awaits us after this life. Yes, it is an important part of our belief system to acknowledge that our friends and family members have gone on to be with God, and are therefore, in "a better place," but we still wonder about them and try to imagine that "better place." Those entrenched in the grieving process are often beset with questions. Where have our loved ones gone? Will we know them when we meet again? Where and how and who will we be after dying?

All Souls' Day helps us to remember that, for Christians, there is no "unbeing"; there is simply "being" in another way: in the spirit, and, we pray, with God. When I was a child, we were taught that on All Saints' Day, we should ask the saints to pray for us; but on All Souls' Day, we should pray for the dead. But perhaps All Souls' Day should be about a little of both. Certainly we want to pray that our loved ones who have died have also gone to be with God, and yet, if that is so, we may also pray to someday join them. All Souls' Day can be a reminder to us that we are not to judge, for only God can judge the life of an individual. No living person can truly know where the soul of a departed person goes after death.

Today, then, is a day to pray for the dead *and* the living. It is a day even to rejoice a little in the good memories we have of those we've lost, and to think about what we learned from those we loved on this earth. Today we may also remember those who have been touched by a recent death and those who are experiencing the anguish of grief and sorrow. Those who are in mourning need our prayers—and even our help—as much as those who have died and are beyond our physical presence and help.

Today is a holy day observed beyond our borders, and extending through many Latin American countries as well. In Mexico, it is called The Day of the Dead, and Mexicans celebrate what seems to be a combination of All Souls' Day, All Saints' Day, and Halloween. They often have processions to cemeteries where they perform rituals to remember the departed; in this way, they observe The Day of the Dead as a festival as much as a solemnity. Perhaps in this there is a lesson for all who live in "the Americas": physical death is a natural part of physical life, and for Christians, the end of the body means a new life for the soul.

PRAYER

ALMIGHTY God, Creator of life, we pray today for those who have departed this life on earth, especially for those we have known and those we have loved. We pray that You bring them to be with You, Lord, so that they may rejoice in Your glorious Presence. We ask also that when our time comes to leave this life, You bring us to be with You, Lord, and with them. While we remain in this life, teach us to walk the path that will lead to You. Father, we pray for those who are mourning a loss at this time. Comfort them and help them to feel the consolation of knowing that You are beside them as they make this painful journey. Amen.

ACTIVITY

DO something today to honor the memory of someone you've loved who has died. Read a card or letter they might have sent you, or the inscription in a book they'd given you.

Wear a piece of jewelry, cuff links, a tie pin, or a piece of clothing they made for or gave to you. Sit in a quiet place and remember the best moment or day or week or year you had together. If you have never lost someone you care about, give thanks to God. Then spend some time with a friend, relative, or acquaintance who is grieving. Give him or her the opportunity to talk about their feelings and their loss. Pray with that person and comfort him or her as best you can.

WE often feel a bit robbed when we have to "change the clocks back," to Standard Time, as if we are somehow losing an hour of daylight. The truth is that the amount of daylight remains almost exactly the same when we "Fall Back" early in the morning on the first Sunday of November; it's just that the dawn comes an hour earlier and so does dusk. Still, we can feel bereft at this event, though historically in America, Daylight Savings Time is a relatively new phenomenon.

Not so long ago, the hours of the day didn't change at all during the year because there was no Daylight Savings Time. In 1895, a New Zealand man who liked collecting insects after work and, therefore, highly valued daylight in the afternoon and evening hours, proposed the idea of Daylight Savings Time to the Wellington Philosophical Society. Originally, George Vernon Hudson suggested a two-hour shift in the day which would allow for the sun to shine even later into the evening. The proposal was met with great interest which was intensified a few years later when a British sportsman and builder, William Willet, also pushed for the concept. Willet was a devoted golfer who disliked having to stop the game at dusk. He also felt that too many people in England's cities slept through the early morning sunlight, and therefore missed an important and productive hour of light. Daylight Savings Time, it was agreed, would effectively, if not actually, "lengthen" the day during the good weather months.

Since then, the 70 countries (and over one billion people) that do "change the time," each have their own method. In America, federal law does not require all states and territories to observe Daylight Savings Time; those that wish to remain consistently in Standard Time may do so. Consequently, some areas of the country that are particularly hot and sunny stick with Standard Time all year, probably because they don't need the extra heat or sunlight. These include Arizona and Hawaii as well as the American territories of Puerto Rico, the Virgin Islands, Guam, and American Samoa. The rest of the country begins Daylight Savings Time early on the second Sunday in March and returns to Standard Time early on the first Sunday in November.

It is a testament to the power of sunlight in our lives that when Standard Time comes around again, we may feel like we're losing something by returning to the norm. Indeed, some in America have pushed for year-round

Daylight Savings Time, noting that the so-called "longer" days of Daylight Savings Time would help people avoid the downward mood swings and the more serious emotional disorders associated with lack of sunlight. The strongest argument for permanent Daylight Savings Time posited a savings in energy consumption and cost due to the fact that people wouldn't have to use as much electricity in the late afternoon and evening. But after some experimenting, America retained the current system, in part because year-round Daylight Savings Time would have forced children to go to school in the dark.

My father hugely resented the return of Standard Time for most of his life. It meant he was going to work in the dark and coming home in the dark with precious little time for his yard and the outdoor activities he loved. But lately, he's taken a different attitude. He sees the advent of Standard Time as a signal to relax, to be patient, to stay inside more and cook more leisurely dinners with my mother. He watches his favorite University of Connecticut basketball teams and Hallmark's month of Christmas movies on television. He is more accepting, more in tune with the slower, twilight season of winter. And, of course, it helps that he's retired and doesn't miss the daylight hours completely.

As my father has discovered, the longer hours of darkness can be an opportunity. We can relax in God's grip, knowing that everything is as He has designed it, and there's a time for slowing down, for resting, for patiently anticipating what is to come. Perhaps the return to Standard Time in America is God's way of helping our fast-paced country, our frantically-paced selves, to relinquish our overwhelming need for control and achievement and acknowledge that only God has power over time.

PRAYER

CREATOR of all time, of every hour, minute and second of every day, we praise You for this "new" time we are experiencing. We thank You for the opportunity to accept that You are in control of us, the earth, and time. Remind us, Lord, that while there never seem to be enough hours in our days, Your time knows no boundaries. Teach us that our measurements of time are a weak substitute for the eternity that is Your time. Help us to rest gratefully, peacefully, in Your shadow. Amen.

ACTIVITY

MAKE a list of all the good things about returning to Standard Time. Granted, you may have to think about it, but there are some! Start with the extra hour of sleep that is the one constant consolation of "Falling Back." List positive things you might do in the twilight hours. Could you spend some time in prayer? Join a book club? Invite friends in for a glass of wine before dinner? Attend a program at your church? Volunteer? Or simply watch the University of Connecticut's girls' basketball team dribble their way to another championship!

ELECTION DAY

TODAY is what it's all been about. The Declaration of Independence, the Revolutionary War, the Constitution, the Bill of Rights, the Emancipation Proclamation, the Civil Rights Act . . . they all boil down to the multi-flavored stew that simmers all day long today. Election Day in America is the intense reduction of its history. Just about every other important date or anniversary in the making of America is, indeed, past history. Today is history in the making.

Election Day in the United States is the day that Democracy actually knocks on the door of every home and asks those inside to come out and play. Today is the day that all the high-flown ideas and eloquent words are translated into action. Today, Americans vote. Every citizen has the right to participate. Every citizen has his or her say in the leadership of this country, and, in some cases on actual questions of government and finances. For the citizens of the United States of America, it doesn't get any better than this.

But as with all things in our great democracy, it wasn't necessarily easy getting here. One of the blessings of America is that voters have the opportunity to vote for many different officeholders in Federal, State, and Local governments. However, that does not make for uncomplicated scheduling. And the fact that voting is the most precious right available to Americans makes it even more important that every effort is made to be sure that every citizen who wishes to vote can do so. Consequently, a great deal of planning and scrutiny goes into establishing schedules and rules for voting. This process has evolved over time and through legislation.

Some of the guidelines for election day are fairly straightforward and apply to every citizen in every state. Federal elections are held in even-numbered years with the President and Vice President elected every four years, while members of the House of Representatives and Senate are elected every two years. Representatives, however, serve only two-year terms while Senators serve staggered six-year terms. States and municipalities may hold elections to coincide with federal elections although they are not legally obligated to do so. Some state and local governments choose to hold state and municipal elections during the same years as local elections to save money. There are careful rules governing other election-related practices as well, including voting by mail, absentee ballots, overseas military ballots, referendums, and recounts. In a few states election day is a civic holiday, and in others, workers are permitted to take time off without losing pay in order to vote.

Much of the law created around election day was based on the fact that America was originally an agrarian society. An election date in early November was necessary because the harvest would have been mostly in and farmers could take the time to vote. Also, early November was usually the quiet before the storms of winter, allowing people who had to travel long distances on poor roads to reach the polls safely. Tuesday was considered ideal because it gave those farmers and travelers a chance to celebrate Sunday, the Sabbath, at home before starting their journey on Monday; also market days were generally on Wednesdays so a Tuesday election date would not interfere with the agricultural economy.

All of this, which may seem like minutiae to us today, is evidence of just how seriously Americans and their leaders have taken the right to vote. The attention paid to every detail indicates an intrinsic understanding that this is perhaps the most important opportunity and obligation for an American citizen. It remains so today, and it is a duty that American

Christians undertake prayerfully and soberly. Political pundits, and even some candidates, have been known to ask, half-jokingly, "What would Jesus do?" about certain political and governing issues. But that is precisely the question Christians should ask themselves as they go to the polls.

PRAYER

FATHER, help us to elect officials who have the same character and spirit You seek. Bring us candidates who reflect Your teachings and the Gospels. Lead us to recognize those leaders who follow most closely to the words and the Spirit of Jesus. We praise You, Lord, for allowing us to live in a country where we can participate at such a basic level in government. Give us the wisdom to make the right choices, the choices You would have us make and not necessarily those we would make guided by our own emotions or fears. Amen.

ACTIVITY

CONSIDER the candidates today with a new eye and in a new spirit. Instead of weighing which candidate will be the best for you personally, perhaps by lowering your taxes or firing/hiring a department head you dislike/like or defeating another country militarily or economically, ask yourself which candidate will be good for the city, state, country, or world according to Jesus' teachings. Which candidate cares about the poor? Which candidate pursues peace and cooperation? Which candidate will "bless" the little children by making sure they are adequately cared for and educated? Which candidate seeks to heal rather than to divide? Think about it. Pray about it. And vote.

DOROTHY DAY'S BIRTHDAY

LIKE the United States of America, Dorothy Day was a little bit of everything. And like the nation she loved, and lovingly criticized, she changed during her lifetime, often shedding her old self like a butterfly sheds a cocoon to emerge as something bright and new. This has been the ongoing story of America, and Day reflected it in her life and choices.

Mirroring America, Dorothy Day was a work in progress, and progression was her byword, geographically, socially, and in her faith. Born into a typical "melting pot" family with a Scots-Irish father from the southern part of America and an English mother from upstate New York, Dorothy started in Brooklyn, New York, and then moved across the country with her family to San Francisco. From there, they went to Chicago, and Day attended two years of college in Illinois before dropping out to return to New York City where she'd been born.

Although she came from a middle class Episcopalian family, from the beginning, Dorothy Day was clearly what one would call different. Even while in college she insisted on supporting herself, despite her father's willingness to help her. This fierce independence would continue to be evident throughout her life. She shunned campus social life and preferred reading radical, socialist works to typical college material. Upon returning to New York City she began to make a name for herself as a social activist and journalist, writing for a number of Socialist publications. One striking difference between Day and her Socialist and Communist colleagues was her commitment to peace. She rejected revolution as a way to bring about the perfect society Socialism envisioned.

In New York, she lived a heady life according to her own rules, engaging in two common-law marriages and choosing at one point to have an abortion. She identified herself as an anarchist and an agnostic. Everything changed with the birth of her daughter Tamar in 1926. Day underwent an extraordinary spiritual epiphany and was baptized a Catholic in 1927. She began writing for Catholic publications and eventually helped establish the Catholic Worker movement and the Catholic Worker newspaper. The movement supported Catholic social teachings and promoted a pacifist position even as the world began to enter the lead up to World War II.

The Catholic Worker movement led to the establishment of communities or "houses of hospitality" where like-minded people lived together sharing their means. Day herself lived in one on Staten Island, and by 1941, over 30 affiliated Catholic Worker communities had been established. Day was called the original hippie, a description she welcomed, and yet increasingly her work among the poor and working-class families gained her respect among Catholics. While she supported women's rights and demonstrated against war, she retained a strong sense of Catholic morality even as she sometimes clashed with the Catholic hierarchy.

To put it mildly, Dorothy Day was a contradiction in terms: an agnostic turned Catholic; a sexually free woman who, after embracing Catholicism, warned against the sexual revolution of the 1960s; a revolutionary who rejected war; a devoted Catholic who questioned Church leaders; a patriot who was uncomfortable with America's capitalism and bellicosity. Like her country she was bold and impulsive, progressive and strong, willing and able to move forward.

In 1983, a mere three years after her death, the Claretian Missionaries proposed Dorothy Day for sainthood, and Pope John Paul II gave the Archdiocese of New York permission to open the "cause" for Day's sainthood in 2000. She was then granted the official title she'd spent her life earning: Servant of God.

PRAYER

PATIENT Father, You are always ready to accept us when we turn to You. Thank You for the example of Dorothy Day, a strong woman who committed herself to You despite making mistakes in her life. We praise You for showing us how You can make us an instrument of Your peace and goodness, if only we let You. Father, let us never believe that our sins and our errors are too great for Your forgiveness. Do not permit us to remove ourselves from the flow of Your love and forgiveness because we are flawed and fearful. As many times as we may turn away from You and Your work, lead us back again. Make us bold in Your service. Amen.

ACTIVITY

IS there something in your past—or even near present—that you regret? Something that may be holding you back as a Christian? Something that is an obstacle to you moving forward, to loving God most fully, to loving yourself and others? Is there something that you need to be forgiven for, but you can't really bring yourself to ask God? He already knows! So take the plunge. Confess. Seek forgiveness. Accept forgiveness. Break the bonds of the past that have been holding you back and forge ahead with God in the lead.

VETERANS DAY,
(REMEMBRANCE DAY, CANADA)

VETERANS Day is another seemingly typical American holiday . . . that does not belong strictly to America. Unlike Memorial Day, when we honor our war dead and which originated in this country mostly around the Civil War, Veterans Day in some form is celebrated in many countries. The date itself takes into account a number of nations as it marks the anniversary of the German signing of the Armistice that ended World War I at the 11th hour on the 11th day of the 11th month in 1918. In some countries our Veterans Day is called Armistice Day or Remembrance Day, as in Canada.

The fact that we share this date with other countries who seek to honor their veterans makes it no less important in America. In fact, it is all the more poignant because it reflects a mutual desire to recognize those who have fought with American soldiers. For instance, President Woodrow Wilson announced the first Armistice Day to be celebrated on November 11, 1919, explaining, "To us in America, the reflections of Armistice Day will be filled with solemn pride in the heroism of those who died in the country's service and with gratitude for the victory, both because of the thing from which it has freed us and because of the opportunity it has given America to show her sympathy with peace and justice in the councils of the nations." Thus, Armistice Day as the precursor to Veterans Day, was intended in part to recognize America and her veterans as part of a world community devoted to the concepts of peace and justice.

Consequently, a great deal of attention has been paid to establishing and defining this holiday in the United States, and it has changed slightly over the past century in its structure if not its purpose. In 1926, the United States Congress issued a resolution asking President Calvin Coolidge to create another proclamation to ensure that November 11 be marked with appropriate ceremonies and services throughout the country, and in 1938 an Act was signed into law making November 11 a legal holiday, "to be dedicated to the cause of world peace and to be thereafter celebrated and known as Armistice Day."

The concept of expanding the holiday dedicated to world peace to include not just veterans who had died during World War I, but all veterans, living or dead, was first put forth in 1953 in Emporia, Kansas. Alvin King, the owner of a shoe repair shop who had been involved with the American War Dads during World War II took up the call to turn Armistice Day into an All Veterans Day, and the people and businesses of Emporia strongly supported this. Their Congressional representative got behind this effort, and President Dwight Eisenhower, a renowned General during WWII, signed a law in 1953 that was amended in June of 1954 to replace the official Armistice Day holiday with Veterans Day.

The federal holiday was again altered in 1971 because of the Uniform Monday Holiday Act which called for certain holidays to be celebrated on a Monday, thus allowing for a long weekend celebration. Veterans Day was moved to the fourth Monday of October, but there was a persistent outcry against altering such a revered day of recognition away from its original date, and in 1978, Veterans Day was returned to its meaningful November 11 date.

The degree of turmoil and controversy over Armistice/Veterans Day reveals how profoundly Americans sought to honor and respect those who serve this country. We wanted to get it right. The attention paid to the holiday also reflects the country's desire to recognize the importance of peace and justice, both nationally and globally. This is a commitment that must resonate strongly with

Christians in America, and all over the world. Jesus preached peace, counseling that human violence had no place in His teachings. As Christians, then, we regard this holiday as a way to honor those who served, of course, but also as a testament to our belief in the power of God's peace over humankind's tendency to war. The fact that the holiday had international origins and a worldwide purpose simply unites us with Christians and peace-loving people all over the world.

PRAYER

JESUS, You told us to love our enemies, and to draw together in Your name. Remind us on this Veterans Day to do just that as we celebrate those men and women who fought in the hope of achieving lasting peace for America and the world. Help us to overcome enmity especially on this day when we celebrate veterans the world over, and unite us in a desire for a world free from war. Bring our national leaders together in that commitment, and teach us to use our vast resources to fulfill it. Amen.

ACTIVITY

MAKE a list of all the nations that America has fought against at some point in its history. It will be a disturbingly long list, and will include nations like England, Spain, Italy, Germany, Japan, China, and Russia, just to name the largest ones. Next list all the ways in which we now work together with many of these nations economically, strategically, and politically. Note the ones we even now consider as strong allies. Finally, list the nations now considered enemies of America and then describe ways in which we may cooperate with these countries in the future.

SAINT FRANCES XAVIER CABRINI'S BIRTHDAY

SAINT Frances Xavier Cabrini may well have been the most humble missionary ever sent to America . . . or anywhere, for that matter! Her desire to be a missionary was so strong that she overcame her shyness in order to imbue her natural humility with a courage that took her far beyond Lombardy, Italy, the place where she was born in 1850, one of thirteen children.

Legend has it that as a child, Frances dressed up her dolls as missionary sisters and, in her imagination, sent them over the water to foreign lands in need of help. Unfortunately, there were no known missionary women in Italy at that time, and when her parents died, she continued to help her brothers and sisters work their farm. Eventually, at the age of 27, she asked the local Bishop for permission to become a missionary for the Church, but the Bishop asked her first to establish an order of missionary sisters. Frances did this willingly, creating the Missionary Sisters of the Sacred Heart to address the needs of poor children in Italy. Nine years later, the order was recognized by the Vatican, and in 1889 Pope Leo XIII asked Cabrini to start a mission in the United States to work with Italian immigrants.

She took six of the sisters from her order and set out for New York City, where they hoped to establish a mission in Little Italy, again, targeting poor children. However, the Archbishop of New York was unwilling to fund it. Cabrini then donned her fundraising "hat," presumably over her veil, and set out to find the money. The wife of a curator at the Metropolitan Museum offered her assistance and soon the Missionary Sisters of the Sacred Heart were helping hundreds of children and families.

Though she had soon established orphanages in Manhattan, Staten Island, Brooklyn, and New Jersey, Cabrini had a dream much like the imaginary play she'd enacted with her dolls all those years ago. She wanted to see her inner city charges playing by a river in the countryside. The Archbishop had apparently learned his lesson about opposing her because he showed her a beautiful Jesuit-owned piece of land north of the city along the Hudson River. The Jesuits had discovered that their well had run dry and they wanted to sell the property. Certain that God would find the water for her, Mother Cabrini acquired the rights to the land. Then she took a long walk. At one point she is said to have stopped, tapped the ground with her walking stick and instructed those with her to dig at that spot. They found water.

By the time of her death in Chicago at the age of 67 in 1917, Mother Cabrini had founded schools, hospitals, and orphanages all over the world. She had crossed the Atlantic Ocean many times and had established more than 60 missions in places like New Orleans, Denver, Seattle, Chicago, Los Angeles, and New York; as well as in Italy, England, Spain, France, and South America. In 1946 Pope Pius XII made her the first American citizen to be canonized.

Frances Cabrini, much like America, overcame her humble beginnings to become one of the most productive missionaries in the history of the Church. Even as she operated at the highest levels of the church and government, she never lost her sense of faith and her commitment to the poor in this country and the world. She recognized that children represent the future, and like Jesus, she insisted that they come to her for comfort and hope.

PRAYER

FATHER, You are the ultimate parent. You are the One Who will never disappoint us, never abandon us, never leave us to our own poor and deeply flawed devices. Thank You for sending us guides like Mother Cabrini, who devoted her life to being a good parent to an untold number of children. Help us to be more like her, with both the children in our lives and the children of the world. Teach us to be the kind of parents who aspire to be compassionate and generous with ourselves and our resources. Lead us to be the champions of children in need in this country and throughout the world. Amen.

ACTIVITY

WITH all that you have to do in your daily life, your work, your routine, your health, your commitments . . . how can you be a champion to a child or children? Try to find time and a way. Can you volunteer at a non-profit for children like the Boy or Girl Scouts, Big Brothers Big Sisters, Unicef, Save the Children, Feed the Children or any number of similar organizations? Can you donate money or goods to one of these agencies? Can you offer to baby-sit for a friend, neighbor, or relative with children? How about running for your town's Board of Education? Can you coach or help with extracurricular activities and clubs at your school system? Find an option that works and "let the little children" come to you.

NOVEMBER 19

GETTYSBURG ADDRESS

SOME historians contend that Abraham Lincoln won the presidency more for his ability to write and orate than for all other factors combined. One proof of this claim is the Gettysburg Address, a speech that was meant to be one small part of a greater program on November 19, 1863, the day the Soldiers' National Cemetery was dedicated in Gettysburg, Pennsylvania. In a little more than two minutes, Lincoln redefined the Civil War from a bloody, gruesome war fought by Americans against Americans to the struggle that would make the future worth living.

Delivered less than five months after Union forces had defeated Confederate troops at the Battle of Gettysburg, a battle that all but ended the Confederacy's chances for victory, Lincoln sought to convey not triumph, but a blueprint for what America could still become in the days after the war. Now thought to be one of the finest speeches in American history, the Gettysburg Address began with those famous words referencing the Declaration of Independence and resulting war for independence, "Four score and seven years ago," and went on to recast the dark days at the end of the Civil War as "a new birth of freedom" for the United

States that would result in true equality for all Americans.

Ostensibly using the speech to consecrate the grounds of a cemetery for all American soldiers, Lincoln went on to extol the virtues of the American ideal, asking all Americans to work to guarantee the survival of these virtues so that the "government of the people, by the people, for the people, shall not perish from the earth." Again, Lincoln returns to this idea of the United States as a grand and wondrous experiment, one that can and must change according to the needs of the people and the time.

In essence, the Gettysburg Address was a short, powerful outline for how America could rebuild and become unified once again after the debilitating years of civil war. It was also an extraordinary articulation of America as a nation founded on Christian ideals and committed to pursuing them at all costs. Slavery had no place in a Christian nation and could no longer be accepted, tolerated, or even ignored. Men and women of God could no longer look away while the words of Jesus were being mocked in an institution that robbed human beings of their humanity.

Perhaps if Lincoln had not fallen victim to an assassin's bullet, the years following the Civil War would have remained true to the national and Christian ideals he so eloquently described in the Gettysburg Address. As it was, his successors had neither the will nor the capacity to pull the nation together and protect the men and women newly freed from slavery. It took a century for Civil Rights to be effectively granted to African Americans and even now, the ugly legacy of slavery still exists in America in the form of racism and inequality in public schools, workplaces, and communities in the south and the north. There is still a great deal of work for those of us who love God, obey Jesus, and believe in the American dream.

PRAYER

JESUS, You came to the earth to be a witness to the truth, to become for all of us, the living Word of God. While human words can be used for good or ill, You have sent Your Spirit to inspire men and women throughout the ages to speak words of truth that reflect Your teachings. Help us to recognize those words and those who speak them. Let us be inspired to do Your difficult work on earth by such words. Strengthen us for the battles that come after wars: the battles for dignity and freedom, decency and equality, peace and prosperity for all. Remind us that no one can truly succeed economically or socially if that success comes at the cost of another's freedom and dignity. Forgive us for the vestiges of slavery that continue in our schools, workplaces, churches, and communities in the form of racism and inequality in America. Teach us how to eradicate it completely, starting with our own hearts and minds. Give us the insight and the ability to create the nation that Abraham Lincoln envisioned and described so simply and so beautifully, so many years ago. Amen.

ACTIVITY

WRITE your own Gettysburg Address. America is burdened today with many problems, among them a growing inequality between the rich and the poor, those who have and those who have not. Frequently, race is a factor in this disturbing trend. Consider what Lincoln faced and the times in which he lived when he wrote the Gettysburg Address. Think about the challenges he sought to address in the speech. Now consider the challenges of racial and economic inequality that we face in America today. Write down your own vision for how America, as a nation under God, should be today. Describe your ideal for this country. Discuss ways to achieve that ideal, or at least move closer to it. Give examples of how we, as Christians, can support and promote equality in America.

NOVEMBER, FOURTH THURSDAY
THANKSGIVING

THANKSGIVING seems to have become one of those love-it-or-hate-it holidays. Some people love it because they see it as a day to gather loved ones around and then cook, talk, and eat and eat and eat. They rejoice in it as the traditional start of the holiday season, and make plans for Christmas shopping on the next day, the Friday that has gone down in retail history as the biggest shopping day of the year. Others see Thanksgiving as a day of obligatory cooking and half-hearted socializing around the television football games, a day that has become about nothing but food and excess, a day when people who have little and are not close to family feel lonely, left out, and maybe even hungrier than usual.

Sadly, few people today seem to see it for what it is: a time to thank God for whatever blessings we've been given.

Our first president, George Washington, made a Proclamation of National Thanksgiving that is seldom heard, but it beautifully captures the purpose and the intent of the holiday: "Now therefore I do recommend and assign Thursday the 26th day of November next to be devoted by the People of these states to the service of that great and glorious Being, who is the beneficent Author of all the good that was, that is, or that will be."

Thanksgiving is celebrated in America and Canada, where the festival takes place on the second Monday of October, the same day as Columbus Day in the United States. It is primarily a North American holiday because it marks the celebration of the first Thanksgiving, a meal shared by early colonists and Native Americans after the settlers had harvested a successful season of crops. These early "Americans" were people powerfully devoted to God who had left England and Europe to avoid religious persecution for their faith.

They were grateful to God for so many things on that first Thanksgiving. A healthy, bountiful crop. An established home and settlement. Peace amongst themselves and with the Native Americans. Good health. And, most importantly for them, the freedom to worship God as they wished to and believed fit. It was a time of thanksgiving as well as praise and rejoicing, and it also mirrored and encompassed the harvest festivals of England and Europe that usually occurred after the agricultural harvest to celebrate bounty and thank God. The Native Americans had similar traditions, particularly those who depended more heavily on crops than hunting.

All of these factors came together in the first Thanksgiving and those that followed, prompting President Washington's reverent Proclamation. From its earliest origins, America—even before we were America—recognized ourselves as a people indebted to a good and gracious God. We recognized and acted on our desire and need to praise, worship, and give thanks to that God in and for everything we had, down to our very survival.

Although that need and desire remains alive in many American homes, it can be easily buried beneath layers of secular traditions, food, football, parades, and revelry. None of these are bad things in and of themselves. But if they are separated from the spirit of thanksgiving to God, they become empty and lead to the gluttony, consumerism, and isolation experienced by some people during Thanksgiving and the start of the holiday season. Thanksgiving is a wonderful reminder that everything we have is from God and He is due our rejoicing and our thanksgiving.

PRAYER

GOD of all that we are and have, we thank You! We thank You that we have being, that You have given us life and permitted us to survive and flourish, each in our own way. We thank You for our families, friends, and loved ones. We thank You for our food, clothing, shelter. We thank You for our books, music, art. We thank You for heat on cold days, clean water, electricity, the means to cook and serve food. We thank You for each other. We thank You for our neighbors, community, church. We thank You for this country which You have favored with abundant resources, caring people, incredible beauty, strong churches, hard workers. We thank You for the freedom to worship You. We thank You for this day in which we are reminded . . . to thank You! Amen.

ACTIVITY

IF you are with family or friends today, pause before your meal and read President Washington's Proclamation of National Thanksgiving. Then, ask everyone present to thank God for something in his or her life (besides the food in front of all of you!), and also to say why he or she is thankful for that particular thing. If you are alone today, come up with your own list of what you need to thank God for and do it privately. Then, call or email someone and let them know that you are thankful for their presence in your life.

SAINT KATHARINE DREXEL'S BIRTHDAY

KATHARINE Drexel was born in 1858, just a few years before the American Civil War, when the subject of the enslavement of Africans was becoming one of the most divisive issues ever faced by the still-young nation. She was also born into an age where many of the Native American tribes had been all but decimated or were fighting for their very existence.

Given the circumstances of Katharine's birth, none of this should have even affected her. She was born into a very wealthy and powerful Philadelphia family, where she might have easily grown to adulthood and even old age untouched by the realities of what many people in America were going through. Certainly, she would have had no reason to attend to the plight of Native Americans or African Americans. By all expectations, Katharine should have led a sheltered young life, married well, borne obedient and well-bred children, and died a rich and proud matron.

But she didn't. At a very young age, Katharine heard and wholly understood the call of Jesus, particularly regarding those who were poor and discriminated against. Despite her many advantages and the age that she lived in, Katharine began to turn her attention, and her Christian focus, onto Native Americans and African Americans. In the tradition of the best and most successful missionaries, Katharine was concerned not only for their spiritual health but for their material and physical states as well. She began her work by donating money to related causes, but soon grew to believe that she needed to be more involved.

Turning her back on the life she might have had, at the age of 33 Katharine committed herself fully to her work. She began by establishing a missionary order, the Sisters of the Blessed Sacrament for Native Americans and African Americans. Over the next century, their influence would spread from Philadelphia to just about every part of America where people of color experienced discrimination and hardship. Seeking the best path to improve their lives, Mother Drexel focused her efforts and her family fortune on establishing educational institutions and opportunities. In 1894, she helped open the first mission school for Native Americans in Santa Fe, New Mexico.

Many more schools bloomed from this first seedling, primarily in the western and southern regions of the country. To ensure continuity, Mother Drexel began to pursue the idea of opening institutions of higher education. In 1915, she established Xavier University in New Orleans, one of the first universities for Black students; it remains today one of the only historically Black, Catholic Universities in the United States. The corps of missionary sisters increased accordingly, and by the time of Katharine Drexel's death in 1955, the order could lay claim to over 500 sisters teaching in over 60 schools in America. In nearly a century of life, Mother Katharine Drexel dedicated most of her years and all of her money, approximately 20 million dollars, to demonstrate the message of Jesus and the power of education to Native and African Americans.

Thirty-three years after her death, Pope John Paul II beatified Katharine Drexel on November 20, 1988, and on October 1, 2000, he canonized her.

PRAYER

ALMIGHTY God, just as You looked down on the oppression of Your people, Israel, under the Egyptians and sent them Moses, so You sent Katharine Drexel and her self-sacrificing sisters to the oppressed and enslaved people in 19th and 20th century America. All over the world, and even still in the United States, Your people live under miserable conditions. They are the victims of racial and economic and tyrannical repression. They suffer, Lord, as You suffer with and for them. Lead us, Father, to be the Katharine Drexels of our world. Give us the courage to lift our minds and our eyes from our own carefully defined lives and look outward at the suffering of others. Give us the strength to be moved beyond our comfort zones to act. Help us to never throw our hands into the air and cry, "What can one person do?" Remind us that history, particularly Christian history, is filled with examples of "what one person can do." Starting with Jesus. Amen.

ACTIVITY

THINK of a time in your life when you felt exceedingly hurt and oppressed by the way others treated you. It may have been in the distant past; it may be right now. You may feel, or have felt, oppressed by an employer, by a lay-off or termination, by your spouse or children or parents, by your church or people in your church, by co-workers. You may be, or have been, hurt or disrespected because of your appearance, your health, your performance at school or work, your mannerisms, your skin color, your speech or language. Whatever the cause, and it may be one that is ongoing and that you will have to deal with all your life, allow yourself to deeply experience the pain and sorrow, perhaps even the paralysis and hopelessness. Understand that in this well of anguish you are joined to people everywhere who feel what you feel. Do your best to use this understanding to develop the empathy and compassion to rise above your own pain and reach out to others who may be unable to help themselves.

MARK TWAIN'S BIRTHDAY

I SPENT 20 years living in Hartford, Connecticut, where Mark Twain is quite a big deal. The large Victorian mansion where he lived for some time and raised his family is a famous museum, part of what had certainly been a radical writer's complex that also included Harriet Beecher Stowe's residence. Like every kid, I'd read about Tom Sawyer and Huck Finn, though I only came to realize much later when I reread the books as an adult that I'd had no idea what they were really about. Living in Hartford I probably came to take Mark Twain for granted. Sure, I toured the house when it was decorated for Christmas, hearing the same spiel from the docent every time; enjoyed concerts and lectures on the sloping grounds; saw his strange inventions and knew all about his bankruptcy. I was so certain that he belonged to Hartford, belonged to me, that I scarcely paid attention to the fact that he had been born in Missouri, had lived all over the country and had been a renowned worldwide traveler.

I expect that just about every literate American feels the same way about Mark Twain, that he's sort of a local guy. And we're all right! Born Samuel Langhorne Clemens on November 30, 1835, Clemens, at various times through the years, lived in or visited just about every part of the United States including both coasts. Unlike other famous American writers who tended to be associated with a particular region—Thoreau and Emerson with New England, William Faulkner with the deep south, Jack London with the west coast— Twain spent impressive chunks of his life in towns and cities all over the country working at a wide range of jobs.

Born in Florida, Missouri, and raised in Hannibal, Missouri, on the Mississippi river where he would set his most famous stories, Twain worked as both a printer and a river-boat pilot. As a young man, he headed west, traveling through the Great Plains and the Rocky Mountains to join his brother, Orion, at a silver-mining settlement in Nevada where he failed as a miner but began to experience real success as a writer and journalist. He then moved to San Francisco and on to the Sandwich Islands which later became Hawaii. His writing, especially his travelogues describing his wanderings, became so popular that he soon went international, visiting and writing about his adventures in Europe and the Middle East, before settling in Hartford.

It is no wonder, then, that William Faulkner called Twain, "the father of American literature." Indeed, there were few places in the country that Twain was not familiar with, and many areas that he visited long before they even became states. For many readers abroad, Twain represented the best of America's literary class, and after he died in 1910, President William Howard Taft noted, "His humor was American, but he was nearly as much appreciated by Englishmen and people of other countries as by his own countrymen. He has made an enduring part of American literature."

Known for his somewhat acerbic wit, Twain's relationship with God was colored by a more self-effacing and gentle humor. Born during the time of Halley's Comet in 1935, Twain said near the end of his life when the comet was due to make another close pass, "I came in with Halley's Comet . . . and I expect to go out with it. The Almighty has said, no doubt, 'Now here are these two unaccountable freaks; they came in together, they must go out together.'" Twain died the next year, April 21, 1910, one day after Halley's Comet's closest approach to the earth.

PRAYER

FATHER, we thank You for giving our country men and women who can both teach us and make us laugh at the same time. Samuel Clemens, Mark Twain, brought this country the gift of humor through his extraordinary perspective and sharp wit while also forcing us to examine the best and worst in ourselves through books like *The Adventures of Huckleberry Finn*. We praise You for sharing his gifts with America, and we celebrate his many travels throughout our country, travels that have given us a window on how others live in these United States. We ask Your blessing on all who are able to see America and her people with clear eyes and who express that vision through writing and art. We ask for the courage to look into the mirrors provided by men and women like Mark Twain. We thank You for the blessing of laughter. Amen.

ACTIVITY

PURCHASE or check one of Mark Twain's books, stories, or essays out of the library. You may also be able to get an on-line version. If you are a Twain fan and have read everything, re-read your favorite. Besides *The Adventures of Huckleberry Finn*, his greatest novels include *The Adventures of Tom Sawyer*, *The Prince and the Pauper*, *Life on the Mississippi*, and *A Connecticut Yankee in King Arthur's Court*. The story that won him initial fame was called "The Celebrated Jumping Frog of Calaveras County." As you read your selected Twain work, consider how it describes a particular region in America. What is your impression of the people from that area and that era? Do you have a sense of what the place looked like? How do you think Twain's description of place and culture at the time the work is set compares to that actual place and culture in America today?

DECEMBER 7

PEARL HARBOR
REMEMBRANCE DAY

ONLY twice in America's history, has it been attacked by a foreign power on its own shores. Most of us have lived through the second attack: the terrorist attack of 9/11. Those of us who did not live through the first attack, the Japanese stealth bombing of Pearl Harbor in 1941, have experienced it through the memories of family and friends, movies, and books. For Americans who actually lived through that fateful day, the pain and amazement will never fade.

For my mother, like many Americans of her generation, Pearl Harbor Day does not seem anything like a holiday. There is nothing for her to celebrate, because until that day, her beloved and athletic oldest brother was headed for a prospective professional career in that wonderful all-American sport of baseball. But when the Japanese government bombed the Hawaiian Naval Base in Pearl Harbor on December 7, 1941, all that changed. Her brother, and many of the young men in the small New England town where they were raised, immediately signed up to go to war. Of course, they had no idea what it would be like.

How could they know, young men barely out of their teens from a tiny town in Connecticut?

But they did what, to them at that time, was their duty. They didn't know what we know today about war and governments and what goes on behind the scenes. They didn't know how much could go wrong in the confusion and chaos of battle. Vietnam, the first "television" war was long in the future. The 24-hour cable news cycle, where anything and everything is blared out over the air waves, was not even imaginable. They had no idea what they were getting into. But they did it anyway, giving up lives and work and girlfriends and new wives and family. Many were leaving home for the first time in their young lives. Many had not traveled out of the state. Many did not come back.

My mother's brother did not come back. Not even his body. He is buried in Tunisia, where, she is comforted to know, the military cemetery is well-kept and immaculate and honored. She has some of his letters, letters from a brave, older brother to a very little sister. In them, he does not complain or look for sympathy. It is clear, reading them now, that he was making every effort to comfort his parents and his sister, to keep them from worrying. And again, how could they know what he was really going through? He certainly didn't tell them. He and his friends were doing their duty. Their duty to their country was to fight to protect it and what it stood for. Their duty to their families was to keep them safe from harm and worry.

Our duty to them, what Tom Brokaw has called "The Greatest Generation" for their commitment to duty, their sacrifices, and their stoicism, is simply one of remembrance and gratitude. On National Pearl Harbor Remembrance Day, we, as a nation, are asked to remember those who were killed on December 7, 1941, in the Pearl Harbor attack. In 1994, the date was established by Congress as a national day of remembrance, and it has become a tradition to fly the American flag at half-mast all day until sunset. As Christians, we can also fly our hearts at "half-mast," honoring, remembering, and praying for the souls of those patriots who lost their lives to help save their country.

PRAYER

GOD of all mercy, we pray that You gather to Yourself the souls of those who have fallen in service to this country, particularly those who died in Pearl Harbor and the subsequent war. Help us never to forget their sacrifice, Lord. Touch the hearts of government leaders in this country and throughout the world. Keep them from the greed, pandering, hatred, rage, and evil that can lead to war. Guide them toward goodness and cooperation. Let them work together unto the good You ordain for all people. Amen.

ACTIVITY

DO something today to honor those men and women who lost their lives at Pearl Harbor and during World War II. Fly a flag at half-mast. Read an article about a World War II veteran or the family of a veteran. Buy or check a book about Pearl Harbor out of the library. Donate to an organization that serves veterans, and enclose a note of gratitude for their work. Send a few Christmas cards with your donation, thanking living veterans and their families for their sacrifice. Light a candle at church or at home and pray for all those who are currently at war or in military service and their families.

DECEMBER 12

OUR LADY OF GUADALUPE*

ACCORDING to tradition the Blessed Virgin appeared to a fifty-five-year-old Aztec Indian Juan Diego, who was hurrying to Mass in Mexico City, on Saturday, December 9, 1531. She sent him to Bishop Zumaraga to ask that a church be built on the spot where she stood. She was at the same place that evening and Sunday evening to get the bishop's answer. After cross-questioning Juan, the bishop ordered him to ask for a sign from the lady who had said she was the Mother of God.

*From *Catholic Book of Novenas* © 2007.

Mary spoke to Juan in these words: "Know and take heed, my dear little son, that I am the holy Mary, ever Virgin, Mother of the true God for Whom we live, the Creator of all the world, Maker of heaven and earth. I urgently desire that a church should be built here, to bear witness to my love, my compassion, my help and protection. For I am a merciful Mother to you and to all your people who love me and trust in me and invoke my help."

Our Lady would give the bishop a sign. She told Juan to go up to the rocks and gather roses. He knew it was neither the time nor the place for roses, but he obeyed.

Gathering the roses into the long cloak worn by Mexican Indians, he returned to the Blessed Mother who arranged them. When he arrived at the bishop's home, Juan unfolded his cloak and the roses fell out. Startled to see the bishop and his attendants kneeling before him, he looked at the cloak and saw there the figure of the Virgin Mary, just as he had described her. The picture was venerated in the bishop's chapel and soon after carried in procession to the first church.

The picture that has aroused all this devotion is a representation of the Immaculate Conception, with the sun, moon, and stars, according to the text in the Book of

Revelation. Mary, clothed in a blue robe dotted with stars, stands on the crescent moon. Underneath the crescent is a supporting Angel. The rays of the sun shoot out on all sides from behind the Blessed Mother.

In 1709, a rich and beautiful shrine was erected near Mexico City; in 1904, it was made a basilica and contains the picture. Pilgrimages have been made to this shrine almost uninterruptedly since 1531. A new and much larger basilica was recently completed. Twenty Popes favored the shrine and its tradition.

The apparition of Our Lady of Guadalupe is Mary's only recorded appearance in North America. Pope Pius XII said, "We are certain that so long as you—Our Lady of Guadalupe—are recognized as Queen and Mother, America and Mexico are saved." He proclaimed her the Patroness of the Americas. The United States was dedicated to the Immaculate Conception by the Third Plenary Council of Baltimore in 1846.

The Image of Our Lady of Guadalupe is the image of the Immaculate Conception. As patroness of Pan-American unity, Our Lady of Guadalupe influences her children to turn toward one another in common love for her and her beloved Son. Because of the close link between the Church in Mexico and the Church in the United States this feast is also celebrated in the United States on December 12.

THE WORD OF GOD

"l have chosen and sanctified this place, that my name may be there forever, and my eyes and my heart may be there perpetually."   —2 Chr 7:16

"You are beautiful . . . , O My love, as comely as Jerusalem, as awe-inspiring as an army in battle array."   —Song 6:4

"Who is she that comes forth like the morning rising, as beautiful as the moon, as bright as the sun, as awe-inspiring as an army in battle array?"   —Song 6:10

FOR THE CHURCH

OUR Lady of Guadalupe, mystical rose, make intercession for Holy Church, protect the Sovereign Pontiff, help all those who invoke you in their needs, and since you are the ever-Virgin Mary and Mother of the true God, obtain for us from your most holy Son the grace of keeping our faith, firm hope in the midst of the bitterness of life, burning charity, and the precious gift of final perseverance. Amen.

FOR OUR COUNTRY

OUR Lady of the Americas, you have blessed our land with your gracious personal visit and numberless miracles, and have left us your own Image as the Immaculate Conception, "Patroness of the United States," and "the Woman clothed with the sun." Be pleased to protect our country from the dangers of war and communism. Help our citizens to serve God faithfully, to respect His holy laws, and finally to be eternally happy with Him in heaven.

Our Lady of Guadalupe, protectress of America, give us peace. Amen.

PRAYER BY POPE JOHN PAUL II

O IMMACULATE Virgin, Mother of the true God and Mother of the Church! You, who from this place reveal your clemency and your pity to all those who ask for your protection; hear the prayer that we address to you with filial trust, and present it to your Son Jesus, our sole Redeemer.

Mother of mercy, Teacher of hidden and silent sacrifice, to you, who come to meet us sinners, we dedicate on this day all our being and all our love. We also dedicate to

you our life, our work, our joys, our infir-
mities and our sorrows.

Grant peace, justice, and prosperity to our
people; for we entrust to your care all that
we have and all that we are, Our Lady and
Mother.

We wish to be entirely yours and to walk
with you along the way of complete faithful-
ness to Jesus Christ in His Church: hold us
always with your loving hand.

Virgin of Guadalupe, Mother of the
Americas, we pray to you for all the Bishops,
that they may lead the faithful along paths
of intense Christian life, of love and humble
service of God and souls.

Contemplate this immense harvest, and
intercede with the Lord that He may instill
a hunger for holiness in the whole People
of God, and grant abundant vocations of
priests and religious, strong in the faith and
zealous dispensers of God's mysteries.

Grant to our homes the grace of loving
and respecting life in its beginnings, with the
same love with which you conceived in your
womb the life of the Son of God.

Blessed Virgin Mary, Mother of Fair Love,
protect our families, so that they may always
be united, and bless the upbringing of our
children.

Our hope, look upon us with compassion, teach us to go continually to Jesus and, if we fall, help us to rise again, to return to Him, by means of the confession of our faults and sins in the Sacrament of Penance, which gives peace to the soul. We beg you to grant us a great love for all the holy Sacraments, which are, as it were, the signs that your Son left us on earth.

Thus, Most Holy Mother, with the peace of God in our conscience, with our hearts free from evil and hatred, we will be able to bring to all true joy and true peace, which come to us from your Son, our Lord Jesus Christ, Who with God the Father and the Holy Spirit, lives and reigns forever. Amen.

Mexico, January 1979

PATRONESS OF THE AMERICAS AND MEXICO

HOW kind you were, O Mary, to appear to an Indian convert in Mexico, leaving on his cloak as credential a permanent image of yourself. You thereby won many for Christ and naturally became the Patroness of Mexico and the Americas, and especially of the poor.

May more and more people through your intercession accept your dear Son as their Lord.

PRAYER

GOD of power and mercy, You blessed the Americas at Tepeyac with the presence of the Virgin Mary at Guadalupe. May her prayers help all men and women to accept each other as brothers and sisters. Through Your justice present in our hearts may Your peace reign in the world. We ask this through our Lord Jesus Christ, Your Son, Who lives and reigns with You and the Holy Spirit, one God, forever and ever. Amen.

DECEMBER 21

FIRST DAY OF WINTER

IN the United States, none of the four seasons reveals our geographic diversity better than winter. Spring is a time of new growth and crop-sowing in just about every state. Summer is relatively warm everywhere. And autumn is universally a fairly unstable period of change and gradually dropping temperatures.

But winter is vastly different in various parts of the country. The states on the Canadian border generally have the most extreme winter weather with a great deal of snow and bitterly cold temperatures. The Mid-Atlantic region has mostly moderate temperatures with the occasional wet or snowy storm. The Southeast is downright balmy most of the time with very little rain. The huge state of Texas alone can have snow in the north and heat waves in the south near the Mexican border. The desert-like regions in Arizona and Nevada can have warm days and cool nights. The West Coast ranges from warm and sunny in Southern California to wet and windy in Portland, Oregon and Washington State. And *wherever* mountains can be found in America, there will be snow. And this isn't even touching upon the difference in winter climates between our two youngest states, Alaska and Hawaii!

As a Connecticut native, I experienced that winter difference twice; once when I spent a winter in Key West, and once when I spent part of December in San Francisco. In Key West, the first day of winter is likely to be between 70 and 80 degrees Fahrenheit and sunny. Brightly colored flowers are everywhere and mangrove trees grow right out of the bath-water-warm ocean water. People stroll around the streets and beaches with sunglasses, shorts, and tank tops. They eat fresh fish at outdoor restaurants under umbrellas and twinkling stars. San Francisco is a bit different. There is a slight chill in the air, though the foggy season has passed. There may be driving wind and rain, but sunlight is just as possible. At Fisherman's Wharf, the tourists move in throngs, dressed in everything from shorts to dresses, suits to work-out attire. Musicians play on street corners for tips and there is a general air of curiosity, excitement, and happiness. Vividly colored bougainvillea flow off porches and trellises. Both places provided quite a contrast from cold, gray Connecticut where I was raised.

Still, there is one common factor on this Winter Solstice, the shortest day of the year everywhere in America. Light. Wherever you may be in the country, you are likely to find a profusion of lights. Often, there will be Christmas lights, strung along houses and trees, on awnings, across stores and office buildings. There will also be candlelight, electric or flickering flames, in windows and on tables. Street lights and lamps will come on early to light the way for pedestrians and drivers. Traffic lights and car lights and construction lights add their glow. Fluorescent lights beam in office buildings for workers who will stay past four or five on this day of the earliest dusk. School lights shine for kids involved in extracurricular activities. Church lights flicker for afternoon and evening services or meetings and, perhaps there will be a spotlight on a crèche.

In Connecticut and throughout New England, lights will come on in houses and cities as people rush through the cold air to reach the warmth of their homes. In Key West, Duval Street will be aglow with tiny lights twisted around giant banyan trees and restaurant porches. In San Francisco, the massive Embarcadero buildings will glimmer with lights so bright they can be seen from across the bay.

This is the response of America to the darkness: let there be light!

PRAYER

JESUS, Lord of illumination, Bringer of light, in the season preceding Your Birthday, we thank You for the gift of light! You are our light in the darkness of our spirits and our days! You are the Light of the world, and You commanded us to let our light shine on others. Help us to do just that on this darkest day and in this shadowed season. Shine the light of goodness on America, in all its diversity and unity, this winter and always. Let us be people of the light in all that we undertake and in all that we achieve. Amen.

ACTIVITY

USING the internet, your public library, or publications on travel, try to find information on various winter festivals in different parts of the country. Learn how people from different regions celebrate the Christmas and winter seasons. From Dickens festivals in San Francisco, to the Christmas tree lighting at the White House, to New Year's Eve fireworks in Las Vegas, to ski holidays in Colorado, to water-skiing Santas in Florida . . . take note of how people all over America celebrate this season and how light in its many forms is incorporated into these festivals.

DECEMBER 25

CHRISTMAS

WHAT is the one word that comes to mind when thinking about Christmas in America. Joy? Praise? Presents? Kindness? Peace? Family? Feasts? Traditions? Tree?

Or is it *STRESS*?

In the media stress is predicted at Christmastime more often than snow. We see articles in major newspapers of how more people are depressed and suicidal at Christmas than at any other time of the year. We read of people getting stressed out because they can't afford to spend what they want to spend, or because they've spent too much and have to face the consequences. Magazines are full of advice for parents and children and families about how to overcome the stress of expectations and familial gatherings that, if they are not outright dysfunctional, are probably at least a bit disappointing. We get advice about over-eating and drinking with dire warnings about the burden such actions place on our bodies, accompanied by previews of diets that can start on January 1.

Welcome to Christmas in America.

How did it get this way? The United States, like its largest contiguous state, Texas, does everything big. So, historically, when Christmas traditions sailed across the Atlantic, particularly those originating in Germany and Great Britain, Americans embraced them. With a vengeance. If Martin Luther could put a small, lit tree on a homely wooden table for his children's pleasure, we could erect massive fir trees in our cities and homes, covering them with more lights and tinsel and gilt than old Martin could even imagine, never mind procure. If Dickens could give us cheerful Christmas spirits who lasted no more than an hour or two, we could produce a Santa Claus who was larger than life and came in multiples. If kids in Europe were happy with a few trinkets and fresh fruit in their stockings, our kids would be bored with rooms piled high with brightly festooned gifts.

Ah, if only we could return to the spirit of that blessed, peaceful first Christmas. Except . . . just how peaceful was it? Joseph and Mary had traveled for days, with her nine months pregnant being jostled around on a donkey and him frantic to find food and shelter along the way, never mind keep her safe from robbers and marauders. The whole country was in an uproar with people leaving their current homes to travel back to the place of their births for the census which, by the way, was just another way for Rome to control and tax them. So, for all their trouble, they'd have to pay out even more. Then when the couple finally made it to Bethlehem, instead of heaving a sigh of relief and enjoying a good dinner with a warm bed waiting upstairs at an inn, they were turned away at every door. So, they ended up in a cave with a bunch of farm animals and really crummy food. And then Mary went into labor.

Talk about stress. And yet from that most stressful time in the life of Mary and Joseph and their nation, came the source of peace for the world. From within the drama of a small family, within the drama of their nation, within the drama of the known world, came peace. Did all of Joseph's and Mary's stress evaporate at Jesus' birth? Probably not. Still, every time they looked into their Son's eyes, they knew it was all worth it. And every time we contemplate Jesus, the Miracle of the Manger in that time of familial, national and global stress, we too can find some measure of peace.

PRAYER

JESUS, You came to us as the literal embodiment of peace in an era of war and fear and anger and oppression. You came into a world rife with economic, geographic, and social tensions. You were born into a time of uncertainty, wandering, and desolation. Lord, we beg You to give us a sense of calm during these days of turmoil and uncertainty in our own lives, our own families, our own nation, our own world. Remind us that we are not the only ones who feel stress, the only ones who suffer, the only ones who live in troubling times. Strengthen us in the knowledge that the only real peace is found in You. Amen.

ACTIVITY

NO matter how stressed or strained or stretched for time you feel this Christmas season, make a commitment to yourself and to Jesus to seek peace. Put aside a few minutes or a day. If you can't make it to a church or some place where a crèche has been set up, then settle in your room or even parked in your car in a quiet place. Imagine yourself in the cave with the Holy Family. Jesus has just been born. The animals are quiet, watching. The shepherds are on the way. The strange and lovely sound you hear is the song of angels and the beating of their wings. You can barely hear it in the quiet. Gaze through your mind's eye on the Baby and His parents. Feel their relief and the tender, awed weariness that has come over them. Let it come over you. Sink down in the clean straw. Draw your cloak around you. Feel the warmth and stillness. Breathe it in. Rest. Rejoice.

DECEMBER 31

NEW YEAR'S EVE

WHEN I was five years old I was terrified of New Year's Eve. Every New Year's Eve my parents would enjoy a rare night out with friends from their high school years. That didn't bother me. In fact, I rather enjoyed the preparations. My father would always make sure that my sister and I had a special meal of our own late that afternoon. We would get to watch Mom select a long, festive skirt and blouse and lay them on the bed for after her bath. Later, she'd put on lipstick and perfume. She'd finish with Jergens hand lotion, always squeezing out a little too much so she could smooth the excess onto our hands and cheeks. I loved that part.

I even liked our baby-sitter. She arrived, rosy-cheeked and smiling, bringing a puzzle we would work on before she put us to bed. My parents kissed us good-bye and then went to the front door. They turned, waving and smiling with amusement at the little joke they were about to make. "OK, girls, see you next year!"

Next year!

They were gone before I could throw myself at them, begging them not to leave us for a whole year! I didn't dare tell our baby-sitter what I was so upset about, fearing that if she found out she was stuck with us for a whole year, she'd leave, too. I lay awake once she put us to bed, trying to figure out a way out of this calamity. Later, much, much later (it probably did seem like a year to me), I heard my parents' car in the driveway. I sat up, silent as the darkness. Soon I heard their voices, low as they spoke to the baby-sitter. It was the sweetest sound in the world. In a few minutes my mother came in and sat on the bed as she always did when they'd been out for the evening. She was flushed with the food and drink and merriment of their night, and she probably didn't think much about why I clung to her like a lifeline in a storm-driven sea.

By the following year, I understood a little more about New Year's Eve, but I still watched my parents leave with just a bit of trepidation. And I've always been a little uncomfortable with the holiday. I invariably feel it is more about something ending than something beginning. It seems to me that America's New Year's Eve celebrations have just a touch of desperation in them, as though we're trying to get something back that we've lost, or are about to lose. I find myself wondering if all the toasts are really about welcoming the New Year, or more about trying to forget what disappointed us in the old one. In our country, it seems we are always looking forward to the next big thing, as if the last big thing didn't quite measure up to our expectations. How many times have we heard people anticipate the New Year by saying, "I sure hope this year's better than last year!"?

One of the great things about God is that He is eternal. We needn't run from the past to be loved and comforted in the present and future. God is constant in His love and forgiveness for us, so we don't have to drown our sorrows or hasten tomorrow to get a new start. Every time we turn our hearts and minds to God, we get a new start. We don't have to worry about whether He's coming home tonight or "next year" because He's already home. God is our home.

PRAYER

LORD, You are our Alpha and Omega, our beginning and our end. In You, there is no weary past, disappointing present, uncertain future. Time as we know it is meaningless to You. You are God, Who was, is, and will be. As this calendar year ends and we find ourselves and our nation stumbling hopefully and perhaps a little frantically into a new one, remind us that Your Presence, love, forgiveness, is unchanging regardless of any calendar made by humans. Comfort us, Lord, with the certainty of Your eternal closeness, so that we need not be afraid of what life might hold in store for us. Help us to put our trust in You, not in the vintage of the champagne, restless resolutions, or a plunging, glitter-covered ball. Let our fear of time be put to rest in Your time-lessness. Amen.

ACTIVITY

CELEBRATE New Year's Eve in what-ever way your plans or traditions dictate (provided, of course, you do so safely). If you usually attend or throw a party, get ready and go. If you gather with a few friends or family for a special meal, get cooking. If you attend a vigil service and then go out for a nice dinner, make the reservations. If you stay home and watch the ball drop from your recliner, put your feet up and turn on the tube. If you stubbornly ignore all festivities, then ignore away. Whatever your plans, follow them with the secure knowledge that midnight doesn't make all that much difference to God. So remember: whether the evening or the year has not quite been what you'd hoped, God is always more than you can even imagine.